THEO MAYEKISO

BEING BLACK

A SOUTH AFRICAN STORY
THAT MATTERS

Published in 2020 by Theo Mayekiso

Copyright ©2020 Theo Mayekiso

ISBN: 978-0-620-89065-6

Cover design & interior crafted with love by the team at:
www.myebook.online

Theo Mayekiso has asserted his rights to be identified as the author of this
work in accordance with the Copyright, Designs and Pattern Act 1998

Published in 2020 by Theo Mayekiso

Copyright ©2020 Theo Mayekiso

ISBN: 978-0-620-89065-6

Cover design & interior crafted with love by the team at:
www.myebook.online

MYEBOOK
WE EMPOWER AUTHORS

CONTENTS

INTRODUCTION

PRAISE FOR BEING BLACK: A SOUTH AFRICAN STORY THAT MATTERS

Theo Mayekiso in his inaugural book, *Being Black: A South African Story that Matters*, opens up his heart, mind and soul in a deeply personal account of his life journey, leading to an intellectual treatment of what 'restitution' could mean in contemporary South Africa. He does this in a warm, affectionate and almost fireside storytelling manner in the first part. He follows this up with an academic analysis of a case study, which attempts to address the vexing question of whether there is a place for white South African men in heaven and attempts of the community of Worcester, a fledgling city in the Western Cape, to find solutions after a racist bomb attack on Christmas Eve, 1996.

One can only hope that what Theo has done with publishing this book inspires others to do the same. We have to tell our own stories, with authenticity and geniuses. Theo has accomplished this with this publication and I predict that many readers, after they have read this book, will feel that they too can do what he has done. I believe that this is what we owe Theo. Let's continue to document our lives, for and by ourselves.

Reflecting on who Theo is and what it is that he has done in publishing this book we can have no doubt that he is a great contributor to our collective narrative in South Africa, particularly as the struggle for restitution continues.

While relating a journey that can only be uniquely his own, simultaneously Theo's story is the story of all disenfranchised people. You have made a wise decision to acquire this book which I do believe will bring great enlightenment while allowing you to bask in the delight of Theo's special storytelling ability.

Enjoy and learn

Noel Daniels CEO, Cornerstone Institute

REVIEWS

This book is very well written and gripping to read. I did not want to stop. It is fascinating and descriptive.

The author is honest and raw, without placing judgements on his childhood experiences, simply telling it like it was/is. For example, how he experienced his parents' ideology and the impact of that. That is so compelling.

The accounts of history are gut wrenching in the way they are told -- I was heartbroken reading more about the impact of colonialism, white supremacy and domination, and racism. It is also clear in the telling of it the impact of these events on today.

To read about South Africa during those years of colonial rule and apartheid through the eyes of a child, is a deep privilege.

There are moments of brilliant humour, and one can be laughing out loud, and minutes later, get hit like a punch in the gut by something unjust that happened or was observed.

The art and power of effective and excellent storytelling is on display in this book. The storytelling is masterful.

I enjoyed seeing the evolution of the author's Christian faith as it changed and matured, as I can see my own journey in his of waking up to a faith and gospel that is holistic and integral.

The book leaves one with a feeling of challenge, a dose of hope-filled reality -- not just reality, and not false 'peace' talk -- but a discussion of hope-filled reality. This is a powerful combination

Every white person I know needs to read this book.

Linda Martindale
Author

I have enjoyed reading this book, and I must say, I am deeply impressed by the efforts and the thinking the author is putting into the restitution.

With racism, and how to be an anti-racist being the topic of many discussions today, this book will help to get an insight into what it feels like to be black in a world of white supremacism and what the best way to combat racism may be. Saying @I am not racist' is clearly not enough!

The world ought to learn a lesson from South Africans like the author, and the BLM activists in the USA should read this book and learn from it too, especially from the discussions at the end.

In a world where individualism reigns, we have seen the effects of it in the growing number of homeless, destitute people, older people left behind in nursing homes, etc. and the EU's handling of the refugee crisis is very doubtful in its morality. The author has shown to me how every European and everyone seeking safety in Europe could profit from an Ubuntu life-style.

The book has a good dose of sudden humour which makes you smile, even while you are moved and saddened about the story. The historic narrations are very educational and help you to understand the history of South Africa.

Roos Demol
CEO
International Community Dynamics
Recruit Refugees Ireland

This is a much-needed book. It is one of those colourful stories of 'ordinary' South Africans who had and are still having extraordinary journeys within the journey of this country. It celebrates being ordinary in an extraordinary way and brings extraordinary insights from ordinary people.

Zinzi Mgolodela
Restitution Foundation

ACKNOWLEDGMENTS

Many people have encouraged me to write this book over many years and for some reason I have never really got down to doing it. However, I started writing this manuscript in 2006 and then I would put it away and then come back to it a couple of years later.

It is only in the last two years that my writing began to gather momentum after I entered the community development space through JL Zwane Presbyterian Church in Gugulethu and VPUU (Violence Prevention through Urban Upgrading).My postgraduate studies in Community Development at Cornerstone Institute also contributed significantly towards the completion of this product.

It would be impossible to mention by name the many individuals who have assisted me in so many different ways in putting this book together but I will mention a few. Thanks to Zinzi Mgolodela one of the executive members of the Restitution Foundation for encouragement and positive feedback after reading the manuscript. I would like to thank

Gianna Maita, my American friend and colleague who read the entire manuscript and made invaluable input and critique.

I am thankful to an old friend Linda Martindale who was able to take time out of her extremely busy schedule to also help proof read and edit the manuscript. Linda also provided me with a great review of the manuscript and she together Wilhelm Verwoerd encouraged me to add another chapter to the manuscript. I am especially thankful to Wilhelm together with John De Gruchy for allowing me to use their material in this book. Roos Demol, my European friend from Ireland offered to proofread/ edit the manuscript and did an amazing job in record time, many thanks to Roos.

I cannot forget to thank the MYeBook team who have been very professional in the way they provided support in the publishing process.

Finally, I would like to thank my wife Thandi who put up with my disappearing acts and long hours in my study and showing a great interest in the manuscript providing help when it is requested. Many of the people who are mentioned in this book are very close to my heart and I want to thank them for being in my life.

FOREWORD

Moderator of the Dutch Reformed Church in South Africa- Nelis Janse van Rensburg

The captivating narrative of Theo Mayekiso's journey from Ngcobo in the Eastern Cape to Worcester in the Boland provides clear and mind shifting perspectives that are necessary to understand the complexity of interracial relationships in South Africa. It is a story of an authentic quest for true reconciliation. The story pushes one towards taking a new position in your relationship with South Africans from different backgrounds than your own.

White South Africans often find it very difficult to understand why black people continue to complain about their racist presuppositions. But white people seldom realize that they only have a white understanding of the realities of society. Their paradigm is white, whether they are conservative or even, to their understanding, liberated from racism and prejudice. Hence, their usual disgruntlement with the dissatisfied black response to their good intentions.

When white people are benevolently trying to help and support black people, they are often left with a distinct feeling that all their good intentions are in vain. All their efforts cannot create true gratitude and recognition, let alone lasting relationships. Over many years it has become clear that closing the gap between white and black communities in South Africa entails more than just being goodhearted or having good intentions.

To cross the divide you also need to have a profound commitment to acknowledge the authenticity and legitimacy of other people's paradigms, backgrounds, assumptions and perspectives although you may not be able to fully comprehend the logic, value or significance thereof. But more than that, as a white person, you need to understand that these are not to be changed or transformed by whites to eventually suit their own preoccupied white agendas. The underlying logic of white ideology is the fallacy that one can be objective and know what others need and how they should conduct themselves

White people therefore first need to understand their own whiteness. They must examine how their assumptions about the world and humanity were formed by a white understanding of everything in life. Unless they obtain a thorough grasp of their whiteness, they will never fully comprehend what it means to be coerced and subjected to it, to conform to whiteness, not out of free will but through the use of power.

The failure to notice the sustained structural racism in our society must be explored and examined too. The popular Merriam-Webster dictionary describes structural or institutional racism as follows: "Institutional racism (also known as systemic racism) is a form of racism that is embedded as normal practice within society or an organization.

It can lead to such issues as discrimination in criminal justice, employment, housing, health care, political power, and education, among other issues." The racial rifts in our nation are begging for a thorough investigation of the rules, norms, routines, patterns of attitudes and behaviour in institutions and other societal structures that represent obstacles to equality. Many presumptions also exist about reversed racism in South Africa. Profound thinking about all of this will position us to build new relationships.

Deconstructing the Western way of thinking within an African context almost involuntary leads one to discern reasons why the blending of cultures is so challenging and out of reach. It will inevitably lead you to individualism as the cornerstone of Western thinking.

Individualism assumes that every person is unique, can make independent choices, can rise above their communities, can have their own way and can do their own thing. Individuals are not necessarily accountable to society, as long as they live within the set rules.

Theo was brought up with the notion of white superiority. His is the story of a black child who had to find meaning in a foreign white world. What made it even more complex was that the black leaders he knew were loyal conformists to white supremacy. He left the rural life of the Eastern Cape without expecting how his deepest understanding of ubuntu *(umntu ngumntu ngabantu)*, meaning I am because we are, which was deeply instilled in his being during his childhood, would be challenged. His subsequent experiences in and outside the church revealed to him the fundamental ideological differences which constitutes the division between the races.

The many rich experiences on his life journey, including his exposure to life in Australia and the United States, provided him with multiple perspectives on Western thinking. He gained clarity about the depth and width of the gaps between the respective ideologies of the South African society and used it to the advantage of the many conversations that were either initiated by him or enriched by his very informed contributions.

It is of paramount importance that white people read this book. They will not only gain much needed insight into their whiteness, but also improve their understanding of the importance and challenges of reconciliation. Although the high tolerance between the different races in South Africa preserved our nation through the most challenging times, we are all worried about the erosion of our common 1994-dream of a reconciled nation.

The time has come to examine the reasons why we so dismally failed to create trust across the societal and racial boundaries of our nation. We are in dire need of trust, not only tolerance. Tolerance alone will not stand the test of time. Trust, unfortunately, will not be achieved by blame placing and self-righteousness. These are the ingredients for the failure of our nation.

This book provides insights that will take our examination to deeper levels of discernment. Trust and reciprocal understanding is a product of free spaces of listening, encountering the worlds of others, learning to be respectful, acknowledging your own blind spots, engaging the pain of your compatriots, embracing each other, moving forward from deep empathy to restorative thinking and exploring ways in which the trust that was gained could be multiplied and structurally embedded in society.

The church, amongst others, has a huge contribution to make to create these spaces and nurture the growth of relationships of integrity. Reconciliation, trust, justice and peace are after all key values of the Christian agenda to create a new world which exemplifies the life to come.

Nelis.

PROLOGUE

Alan Paton's great novel "Cry the Beloved Country" starts with these words: There is a lovely road that runs from Ixopo into the hills. These hills are grass-covered and rolling, and they are lovely beyond any singing of it. This reminds me of the rolling hills of the Transkei where I was born. Besides Ngcobo, which is my hometown.

I have spent several years in Willowvale where I worked as a principal of a Bible school. The town has a population that numbers only in the few hundreds, but also played a rather pivotal role in Transkei's history. It was in this area that the local Xhosa split into two factions. The senior section remained in the Willowvale area while the split-off group moved to the south, beyond the Kei River.

The British invaded the land of the Gcaleka in 1837 and settled 40 000 Mfengu tribesmen in the area. Trouble broke out Immediately between the residents and the new settlers, which led to the Ninth and final Frontier War in 1877. The Xhosa were defeated at the Battle of Kentani and the bulk of the Gcaleka people were driven north. This, combined with the decimation

1

of the Xhosa people after the prophecy of Nongqawuse, led to the area becoming almost completely de-populated.

The little mission station that had been built at Willowvale and named after the row of willow trees behind the mission, was abandoned. One Saturday morning, I was driving on a rather rugged road that connects Willowvale with Butterworth a town that was once the industrial hub of the Transkei. Butterworth is the oldest town in the Transkei, built quite near to the place where the great chief Hintsa had his palace. Methodist missionaries founded it in 1827. The Xhosa name is Gcuwa after the river running through it, but the English name is from the then- treasurer of the Wesleyan Mission Society, Reverend Butterworth. At the end of the Frontier Wars – during which the town had been burnt down three times - traders began to settle here. During the days of 'independence', it was earmarked as a site for industrial development but most of these ambitious projects have now been abandoned.

David, my then seven-year-old son was keeping me company and we were having serious conversations.

I cannot remember what we were talking about, but I do remember that as we were descending slowly towards a stream just past Nqadu Great Place where the Royal Palace of the Amaxhosa is located, there was a vehicle travelling in the opposite direction, and we could clearly see that the driver was white.

Since the bridge was small and only one vehicle could pass at a time and I was the one closest to the bridge I expected the driver of the oncoming vehicle to give me the right of way. I was not sure if he was going to do that because he was travelling a bit fast. I said to David "I hope this man stops and allows me to go first."

I was not expecting a response from David but then David warned innocently "But daddy, white people always make wrong choices. ". I could not argue with that and fortunately, our 'friend' on the other side of the bridge made the right choice and stopped! I have no idea where David learned that. He attended a multiracial Crèche when we still lived in Somerset West in the Western Cape and then went on to attend Somerset West Primary school which was a so called model C school (once a whites only) then we relocated to the Eastern Cape when the Cape Town atmosphere really suffocated me.

There is another little incident that I remember when David was still at Pre School. I had come to pick him up and as we were heading towards the door, one of the little ones started laughing aloud. He had a light complexion so he would be classified as coloured. This laughter irked little David, whose mother was coloured, and he turned around and said to the little oak "Don't laugh your father is also black."

I so wish that this book was not about race. I wish I could tell my story without mentioning race but then it would be a denial of the fact that I am a social construct. I wish I could look at life the way Sabina does."I don't understand why South Africans have to always see things through a racial lens." She sounded genuine and sincere and could not understand why she would be labelled as white.

I think Sabina knows that being white in South Africa is not just about one's complexion; it is about what you represent. Sabina, a petite Italian born blondish or strawberry blonde, as she would describe herself, mother of two is passionate about making a difference in people's lives in South Africa. "I came here because I wanted to deal with society." She states this emphatically as she moves in her seat rather restlessly. She then removes her glasses to give me a gaze.

I had always thought of Sabina as an architect and an urban designer and so I wondered why an urban designer would hope to impact marginalized communities. Then Sabina explains that apartheid spatial planning, which she says, in the case of South Africa fascinated her, it is not an exception, but it is extreme. Her PhD Thesis was on Mapping Social Spatial Exclusion. I think Sabina would like to be known as a Development Practitioner or a development activist instead of being labelled white and therefore carry all that whiteness represents in South Africa. Sabina does admit that she grew up in a place in Italy where there was no diversity of races but had a yearning for it.

However, a case can be made that the reason white people do not want to talk about race is because it's an uncomfortable subject. One of the reasons could be a simplistic understanding of racism. It could also be what Robin Di Angelo calls "White Fragility."

I am never sure about letting people like Sabina off the hook. Nevertheless, as South Africans we cannot afford not to have the type of conversations that will liberate us from our dark past of colonialism and apartheid. We are carrying a burden brought upon us by history and many of us thought that after 1994 the burden would simply fall off our shoulders and we would be free.

We were naïve enough to think that a new political dispensation would deliver a new order.

The aim of this book is to help all South Africans and perhaps white South Africans in particular to understand that black pain is a reality and is being experienced by black people on a daily basis, and also for black people to face up to this reality and not be in denial about it; whether one was born in an urban or rural setting.

Our white compatriots must learn to listen to and co journey with fellow black compatriots. We cannot just simply move on while the pain that has been inflicted over three centuries is deepening inside many inhabitants of this beautiful country.

I was born in a remote part of the country and, unlike David, when I was his age, my greatest ambition was to shake a white man's hand and that is where my story begins. It is about pain, exclusion and a quest for justice.

This book is divided into four parts.:

The **First Part** is entitled **"Being Black: My story".** It is my story and is meant to frame a broader conversation about racism

The **Second Part** has the title **"Being White: De Gruchy and Verwoerd."** It is about white males confronting racial injustice through a memorial lecture and a response to it.

The **Third Part** with the title **"Social Restitution: A journey.** "This is meant for people who may want to go on a social restitution journey.

The **Forth Part** is **"Voices from Worcester: A Dream"** is part of my research theses on social restitution in Worcester. This section is intended to get people talking about structural racism, restitution and social restitution in particular.

25 July 2020

PART ONE

"Being Black: My Story"

CHAPTER ONE

Sometime in 1974, the rumours of a looming war spread in the quiet village of Gotyubeni, which falls under the magisterial district of Engcobo in the Transkei. The South African government set up the area as one of the two homelands for Xhosa-speaking people in Cape Province, the other being Ciskei; it was given nominal autonomy in 1963

Engcobo is roughly halfway between Queenstown and Umtata along the R61. It was established in 1876 when Walter Stanford arrived at the nearby mission of All Saints Station to take up his appointment as the Resident Magistrate to the Amaqwathi – the town is 8km from the mission station.

Engcobo is endowed with natural beauty and can be called the jewel of the Eastern Cape. The area has earned itself a reputation of being a place of thieves (Emaseleni).

For one to understand where this comes from, one must first understand what the name 'Ngcobo' means. It means a green place next to a stream. Therefore, Engcobo being fertile and lush means that it naturally attracted livestock long before it was a magisterial district. Livestock tended to remain there and would then find or be found by new owners.

People of Engcobo would explain that this was not theft, as others would tend to believe. It was an act of compassion towards stray animals that got misunderstood. If you visit Ngcobo, which is now a town, it is clear that livestock would thrive in the area.

There is an interesting link between Ngcobo and Mjanyana, a leprosy and TB hospital located adjacent to Gotyubeni, my home village which is some 35 km away.

For a bit of background, Mjanyana never started as a hospital. Ngcobo was established in 1876 as a magisterial town. In 1879, the Amaqwathi rose in rebellion and during the ensuing hostilities both the mission and the magistracy were burnt to the ground, forcing their residents to flee.

It was then that Stanford relocated his magistracy to Mjanyana. for a period of about 2 years, Mjanyana was the magisterial seat of Ngcobo.

It was 1894 when the Society for the Propagation of the Gospel in Foreign Parts (SPG) established a mission and a lazaretto there.

There is a period of about 14 years after Stanford relocated his magisterial seat back to Ngcobo and the establishment of the mission and lazaretto in Mjanyana. One is left to wonder what could have happened in Mjanyana between 1889 and 1894.

In the 1970s Mjanyana was a thriving farm that boasted a large herd of Friesland cows in addition to the leprosy and TB hospitals.

A feared white man who was nicknamed 'Xhomiyaka-yaka' by the locals ran this farm. It is difficult to know the origins of the nicknames that locals would often give to white people. In almost all cases, they describe something about the character or behavior of the person concerned.

Xhomiyaka-yaka means "*hanging up a shredded piece of cloth*". Usually these names have the potential to anger the people that they are directed to, so they become a well-known secret.

It is probably worthwhile to know something about Walter Stanford who started the town of Ngcobo. Walter Ernest Mortimer Stanford was born on 2 August 1850 in Alice. His grandparents were part of the 1820 settlers. His father, William Stanford, was born in 1820 shortly after the arrival of the settlers; his mother was Mrs. William Wright. The couple had three children, Robert, Walter and Arthur. When Stanford was six years old, his father was killed in a riding accident. Subsequently, in 1857, he was sent to live with his uncle J.C. Warner, a missionary in charge of the mission at Glen Grey in Queenstown.

The reason for this was that Stanford was sickly and his mother hoped that by sending him to live in a place of higher altitude his condition might improve. Stanford spent the following three years with his uncle being educated by Aunt Mary Stanford. In 1860, Stanford moved back to his mother in Alice and spent the next two years of his education at the Lovedale Mission Institute.

At the age of twelve, he ceased his formal education. Stanford began working as a clerk for his uncle in July 1863 under the Department of Native Affairs in Glen Grey. During his uncle's absence, he became the Tambookie agent. In 1869, he spent some time working as a bookkeeper before returning to the Department of Native Affairs. Due to his good work ethic and ability, Stanford was able to advance steadily and by 1876, he was appointed magistrate with Dalasile, the chief of the AmaQwati.

During the Ninth War of Dispossession, Stanford was appointed to oversee the division that collected levies from African people to fund the Gcalekaland campaign (Frontier War). At the end of the campaign, Stanford returned to his work at Ngcobo.

Ngcobo was a town some 35 km away from my village and was only visited by adults either for shopping or to visit some government offices and deal with court-related issues. Nkobongo, a beautiful and elegant forested mountain, was a big physical barrier between my village and the town. We knew that on the other side of the mountain was a place where white people lived. We had heard many stories about this strange race. Most people in the village had worked for them at some point in their lives.Some would come home once a year for their holidays, either from the then Orange Free State or the Transvaal. Our province was part of the Cape Province. They would tell stories about the cruelty, ill treatment, and brutality that they sometimes experienced in these faraway places from their white hard taskmasters. It seemed to us that they always came back better off.They would come back with nice clothing and sometime driving their own vehicles. I remember that the vehicles never used to last and, in most cases,, they would go back to work without them. I think it is fair to say that my father was a fan of white people.I think he never quite knew where to place them. He would talk proudly about how he had learnt to speak Afrikaans, thus creating a ladder for him to become a supervisor at his factory. He believed that one must do everything to endear oneself to white people. He would sometimes say "*Abelungu banengqondo* " White people are clever. I honestly cannot remember in what context my father would say those words. He did once tell us when we were children, about a rather horrific story; a day that he and my mother could not forget.

"Your mother was very scared that day", my father told us half amused as he stared at my mother. We were sitting around a Falkirk coal stove on a cold winter evening, as we usually did. Our family of ten used to have conversations about all manner of things.

This story was about one Saturday afternoon when white officials entered their compound to check if their documents were in order. Apparently, many of the workers' documents were not in order and they were beaten up. You could hear screams coming out of this home, the treatment was brutal. As they were about to enter my parent's little yard, one of the officials shouted "Stanley se huis!"

They immediately skipped the house and went to the next one. If they had not done that, my mother would have watched her husband being beaten up and she would have been next in line. I have often wondered why my father's house was left untouched by these brutal rascals. Could it be that he was an *"impimpi."* (Informer). Knowing my father the way I do, I do not think he would have ever been capable of selling his colleagues out. There might have been pressure for him to do so, which was probably the reason for him to leave and venture into an uncertain world of business in the Transkei.

My father was hardly ever at home. Being the only breadwinner, he would go out trying to find livestock to either sell or slaughter for our butchery.

Sometimes he would travel to the then Free State, visiting farms where there were livestock sales or auctions. He could not afford a decent vehicle that could travel far. He would walk long distances between farms as he hunted for the best deals.

On one occasion, on a very cold winter's night, he had to sleep under a tree in the middle of nowhere because it got dark before he reached the next farm. "I had to" my father explained, "Otherwise the Boers would have shot me if I entered their premises at night."

My father's business was located in the deep rural Transkei. Prior to being a struggling businessperson in the Transkei, he was a factory worker in the Boland town of Wolseley, in the then Cape Province of which Transkei was a part.

He had spent the better part of his life working in factories in Wolseley near Cape Town; he learnt to speak Afrikaans and became his bosses' favourite.

He then became a "makhulu boy", who oversaw the other 'natives', as they were then called. My father lost three of his fingers because of an accident while at work and he was never compensated for that. The company he worked for was called Langeberg.

The company told him that black people normally cut their fingers off as a tribal ritual. When he insisted on being compensated, he was given a few cans of canned vegetables by the canning company.

My mother was a domestic worker, cooking and cleaning for her white employers in the same town.

She used to tell us that there was a place in the Bible that says that black people are under the curse of Ham and will always be subservient to the white race. Of course, one did not have to look hard to believe that. I later learned that what my mother was referring to was the Ham Theory, which is rooted in some Christian Theology.

My parents decided in 1960 to relocate to the Transkei when the territory was given a self-governing status by Pretoria. They then settled in Ngcobo in the village of Gotyubeni, which is where I grew up. The closest hospital was All Saints, about 8 km from the town of Ngcobo. I was born in July 1965, four months before time.

As a premature baby, I was kept in an incubator for four months. I was the first of my mother's children to be born prematurely. She had six previous deliveries, which were eventless, and so mine was a new experience. Apparently, no one expected me to survive, except my mother and perhaps the doctor.

The issue of giving me a name also came up. How long should they wait before giving me a name? What should the name be? My father suggested that I would be called Zolani, which means 'be calm'. My mother rejected this suggestion because it sounded like giving in. Her choice of name was Thembinkosi, which means 'trusting in the Lord'. She would talk about how she used to walk to a solitary place outside the hospital premises to pray. The doctor, a certain Dr Eglin, also entered the fray by giving a Christian name. He explained to my mother that premature babies are 'very special' and Theophilus would be a fitting name for me. I ended up being called Theophilus, which means God's friend or the beloved of God, and Thembinkosi. Both my names have God in them! I actually feel that I would have preferred the name Zolani.

People who know me also think that Zolani would be more descriptive of my nature. However, I also do trust the Lord. Some of my siblings are deceased, namely Posi and Simo. I now have one brother, Mangena and four sisters: Nomalanga, Thandiswa, Kholeka and Nomfundo.

In 1960, when my parents relocated, their main motivation was to start a business, as the Transkei was the only place where black people of the then Cape Province could run their own businesses. I believe that my father could have run a highly successful and profitable business if conditions had been favorable. He was quite passionate about what he did and was a hard worker, which is probably why the white people liked him so much.

Back to the rumors of war. During the years 1974 and 75 we began to hear that Transkei was going to be independent of South Africa and that the Pretoria regime was opposed to that. We heard that our great leader, the Chief Minister of Transkei, Chief Kaiser Daliwonga Matanzima (affectionately known as KD), wanted his people free from the white yoke of oppression. Our little minds as children could not quite comprehend or fully grasp the notion of freedom and independence.

This message had an appeal that could not be resisted. I never wanted to believe my mother when she said that, according to the Bible, our place in the world as the black race was that of servitude. My father's often-made comments that the intellect of the white race was superior to that of the black race never sounded right.

The stories that I had heard from migrant workers while on leave often bothered me. I wanted KD's independence. I wanted freedom, I wanted equality, I wanted fairness, I wanted justice, I wanted dignity. I wanted...No, I did not want ... war. I understood war to be an undesirable consequence of serious conflicts between nations.

At that time I was not even aware that some 86 years before I was born, in the year 1879, approximately 80 km from where my family lived, the ninth and the final war of dispossession took place. It was one of the wars that are sometimes referred to as Frontier Wars, but I think Wars of Dispossession is a more fitting term.

The Amaxhosa fought the so-called Frontier Wars against the British invaders, over a hundred-year period. The plan as outlined by one of the Governors of the Cape, Sir George Grey, was 'to break up the Xhosa nation entirely. It is to lose its home and its culture. It is to be scattered to the furthest reaches of the Colony and never to go back again.'

Grey made no bones about the grand colonial plan for the Amaxhosa. They were to become 'useful servants, consumers of our goods, contributors to our revenue.'

The bitter wars of dispossession had left the once proud nation bitter and broken. The great King Hintsa was brutally murdered by Governor Sir Benjamin D'Urban and his gang in April 1835, when he tried to escape from capture. On the day, Hintsa rode proudly into the camp of the Governor after he was given personal assurances of his personal safety, but he was never to leave the camp alive.

D'Urban disarmed Hintsa's retinue, placed the King under heavy guard and threatened to hang him from the nearest tree. Hintsa was held hostage for a ransom of 25000 cattle and 500 horses, 'war damages' owed to the Colony. When he tried to escape, he was shot down and his ears were cut off as military souvenirs.

My ancestors put up a fight and fought fiercely against colonialism and dispossession over a period of one hundred years!

Chief Maqoma, the greatest military commander that the Xhosa nation has ever known, fought in five of those wars. Sir Harry Smith once ordered Maqoma to his knees and, placing his gubernatorial boot on the chief's neck declared, 'This is to teach you that I am come hither to show (Xhosa land) that I am chief and master here'. Chief Maqoma is said to have responded by saying 'You are a dog (alluding to Smith's low birth) and so you behave like a dog. This thing was not sent by Victoria who knows that I am of royal blood like herself.. After some of Harry Smith's ceremonies , chiefs would be required to kiss Smith's boots and shout '*Inkose' nkulu! Inkose'nkulu!*' The great chief! The great chief!

JEFF PEIRES, A RENOWNED HISTORIAN, RELATES THE FATE OF SOME OF THE AMAXHOSA CHIEFS INCLUDING CHIEF MAQOMA:

One by one, the Xhosa chiefs served out their sentences. In 1869 the last prisoners, Maqoma,Siyolo and Xhoxho were released. On their return home, they found their land lost and their people scattered. They were forbidden to own land or to summon their followers. Maqoma, in extreme old age, refused to abide by the regulations imposed on him. Twice in 1871, with no aim at defiance but defiance itself, he left his appointed place of residence and returned to his old lands near Fort Beaufort and the Waterkloof. He was easily captured, and on the second occasion, he was summarily returned to the Island without a hearing or trial. This time he was alone, utterly alone. He never saw a visitor and there was no one else on the Island who spoke any Xhosa. Even the goats, which he had formerly kept, were dead. When in September 1873 he started sinking after 18 months of solitude, the Island authorities sent for a companion and interpreter. Nevertheless, it was too late. This most brilliant of Xhosa warriors cried bitterly, according to the Anglican chaplain who witnessed his last moments, before he passed away 'of old age and dejection, at being here alone-no wife, or child, or attendant. Four years later, the last Frontier War broke out. The sons of Maqoma, Mhala, and

Sandile were among the first of the next generation to take their places on Robben Island.

When I was young, the only weapon of war I had seen was an old rifle that my father owned and kept under his bed. It had no bullets. I doubt very much that it worked. We made sure that the village knew we had this weapon, so they knew we were not to be messed with!

Oh yes, the white police officers would sometimes come with their revolvers clearly visible, when an arrest had to be made. The police were never our friends. I still have vivid pictures of the white Landrover pick-up vans that used to be driven at high speed through the village with very long antennas protruding through the air. The police officers would be white, well-built, with a big moustache and fierce looking, and would mostly be accompanied by a black police officer who always looked timid and bent on pleasing the master. We believed that the antennas could pick up our private conversations, so when the police were around, one had to be careful what he said. The whole set up was designed to intimidate whoever wanted to challenge the status quo.

The rumours of war kept spreading and we were informed through our school that the Chief Minister would be visiting our village. The school made sure that a special choir would sing songs that praised the Chief Minister. It was within a matter of days that the big gathering took place at Chief Bazindlovu's kraal of the abaThembu clan. The Thembu tribe reaches back for twenty generations to King Zwide. According to tradition, the Thembu people lived in the foothills of the Drakensberg Mountains and migrated toward the coast in the sixteenth century, where they were incorporated into the Xhosa nation.

The Xhosa are part of the Nguni people who have lived, hunted and fished in the rich and temperate southern region of South Africa, between the great interior plateau to the north and the Indian Ocean to the south, since at least the eleventh century. The Nguni can be divided into a northern group - the Zulu and the Swazi people - and southern group, which is made up of amaBaca,amaBomvana,amaGcaleka,amaMfengu, amaMpondomise,amaMpondo,Basotho and abaThembu. Together they comprise the Xhosa nation.

The first democratically elected president of South Africa, Nelson Rolihlahla Mandela, came from the Thembu clan. He was also an uncle to KD Matanzima.

But back to the day the Chief would visit our village. The elderly, adults, teenagers and children, even the dogs, came to this gathering. Some drove, some rode horses, others cycled or walked, but they came. This was indeed a great day; we were going to know the true situation.

After the singing was done, the Master of Ceremonies introduced the Chief Minister. Many of us had never seen him before and could hardly guess who he was among the dignitaries seated on the stage.

As soon as he was introduced, a man in a black suit jumped up from among the dignitaries. He had a large physique, deprived of height and middle aged, he talked easily and fast. In his hand he had a short, beaded stick that he waved about rather furiously. He said many things that I could not comprehend.

The older folks among the audience were getting excited. The man had the audience with him, there was laughter, cheering, clapping and even loud shouts of agreement, women were ululating. For a while I thought this man was the Chief Minister and that we were in for a good time. I was starting to get excited myself when the man suddenly stopped and bowed out of the stage. I later learned that this man, a certain Mr Matiwane, was a praise singer. As he bowed out there was already a tall, immaculately dressed gentleman with piercing eyes on the podium, looking very serious.

I could see that this was not the kind of person one could mess with. I was totally convinced that this man was there to spoil the fun. He had no reason to intimidate our 'Chief Minister', so I thought.

While all these thoughts were going through my mind, the crowd saluted in unison "Ah Daliwonga!!!" The man's lips reflected a smile while his face remained serious.

KD's royal palace or Great Place, as it is normally referred to, was in Qamata near Cofimvaba. The capital of the Transkei territory where he ruled from, was Umtata. Many believed that KD had magical powers that enabled him to transform into an animal so that he could escape from his many enemies. I did not know then that he had enemies.

KD began his address by confirming our worst fears. He informed the audience that the rumours of war were true. *"Abelungu abafuni nenkululeko"* (White people do not want you to be free). "War is inevitable!" he boomed and then paused to allow the crowd to grasp the gravity of the situation. While he paused, his already serious face stiffened. The silence was deafening.The audience had now been transformed into a sea of despair. "But …," the Chief Minister interrupted the silence. "You don't need to fight," he declared.

This statement stunned everybody. "I will fight for you." All eyes were now fastened on him questioningly and maybe admiringly. "I have my weapon." As he said that, he lifted his right hand up towards his chest, reached for his pen on the left upper pocket of his stunning suit, and showed the audience the pen. "This is my weapon," he said slowly.

Then the crowd erupted in a rare display of excitement, admiration, relief and even awe, and shouted. "Ah! Daliwonga!" As a nine-year-old, I was ecstatic. I felt extremely proud to have KD as my leader.

I cannot recall what most of his speech was about, but I do remember that he kept mentioning some of his enemies whom he called *"amagiyo-giyo"* (African Pied Starling). I assumed that those people were white; I later learned that KD's enemies were not necessarily white. There was a section of society that regarded him as a sell-out and *"Hlohlesakhe"* (the one who fills his own stomach first).

That day was a great one for me. It was my very first exposure to homeland politics. I remember relaying the events of the day to my father, who had not been able to attend, with great enthusiasm.

On the 26th of October 1976, the self-governing territory of the Transkei became independent of South Africa and was declared a Republic. Those that were fortunate enough and had the means to travel went to Umtata where the great event took place. The rest of us were informed of the proceedings via a newly formed radio station that became known as Radio Transkei.

As a young boy at boarding school in Mthatha, I hardly ever missed Matanzima's rallies. He once declared at a rally that people must only listen to him because he was the only one that was intelligent, and as an afterthought he said, "And my younger brother Chief Mzimvubu."

Matanzima once told a story of a group of angry men who travelled by train from Cape Town to the Transkei. The trip, he stated, took three days, a distance of more than one thousand kilometres. When they arrived in Transkei still furious, they were asked what they were looking for. "We want to kill uMatanzima!" People asked why they wanted to kill uMatanzima. And their answer was "UMatanzima has sold the nation."

"For how much?" was the question that followed. The angry group could not answer this question. Matanzima would tell this to the great delight of his audience.

When I was about 13 years old, I ended up living in the actual town of Ngcobo. My arrival in the town was unplanned and unceremonial. It was frankly, a scary adventure!

I could no longer stand the abuse I was receiving at school through corporal punishment. My feeling was that teachers had been given unrestricted powers over us, which they could exercise at will. There was no recourse and the teachers were always right.

I was forced to join a choir practice in preparation for an upcoming Choir competition. Mr Mbulawa, known as Gxara, seemed to enjoy inflicting maximum pain on us whenever a note was missed. I used to miss many notes and payed dearly for it!

My father felt that education would be the only way to escape poverty and ensure a better future. I knew that he would never allow me to quit school and stay at home. I thought there was only one option – to run away!. The idea was to join other run-aways from the same village. Most of them had run away for similar reasons.

Ngcobo was a small town, so it was not difficult to find the friends from my village. I was actually looking for one particular friend who was a bit older than me and came from a worse-off family. I found Mpendulo squatting together with a few other boys in the backyard of Wick's Supermarket.

Wicks was the equivalent of the Spar today, with supermarkets in many towns of the Transkei. It was owned and run by whites who chose not to leave the Transkei after Matanzima's independence. Mpendulo and the other boys were unemployed and living off waste food from this supermarket.

The conditions were pathetic, to say the least. Mpendulo was surprised to see me because my father was once his boss and he used to do gardening at our home. I think he was also happy to see me and he introduced me to his friends.

I was now destitute, facing an uncertain future in a shack behind Wick's supermarket. But I felt good about being away from home and away from Mr Mbulawa my choirmaster. It was great to know that I would never have to face him again.

I decided to find a job together with my friends and carve out a new future for myself.

After a few days, Mpendulo shared a secret recipe for success with me. He told me that I needed to get lard (rendered pig fat) and white man's hair; mix it, then fry the hair a bit. This, he explained, would be an ointment to rub on my face before job hunting so that the white people would just love me and offer me a job.

He shared that getting pig fat was not a big problem, but getting a white man's hair was a huge challenge. "Where does one go to find white man's hair? They do not go to our hair salons!" He exclaimed hopelessly.

Ngcobo, Stanford's town, had not grown much since he established it some 86 years before. The magistrate's office was much bigger than it was before due to population growth and an alarming increase of social ills. Whites and a smattering of black households mainly populated the town, thanks to Matanzima's independence.

Yes, the black middle class were making their presence felt. In the middle of town was a large BP garage run and owned by Mr Titus, a thriving black entrepreneur. The garage, known as Bashee Motors, boasted a state-of-the-art showroom with the latest range of Toyotas. It was also equipped with a state-of-the-art workshop. Mr Titus was probably the most prosperous black entrepreneur in town. Other blacks who also seemed to be doing very well in this town, judging by the types of houses they had and the cars they drove, were medical practitioners.

Mr Nyamakazi was also a successful entrepreneur in the town. Across the road from Mr Titus' Bashee Motors was a large house with colonial architecture. The Ndunganes, a middle-class family of three, owned this house. Mr Ndungane was the deputy principal at Daliwonga Senior Secondary School, named after KD, near Cofimvaba. Mrs Ndungane was a nurse at All Saints Hospital where I was born.

Their only child was a girl called Lindelwa who was a student at Ndamase State High School near Nqgeleni in western Pondoland, approximately 32 km southeast of Mthatha.

The Ndunganes lived a comfortable life and were devout Anglicans. I later learned that they were closely related to Njongonkulu Ndungane who became the archbishop of Cape Town. The Ndunganes also had two domestic workers who were accommodated in the large house. One of them was a beautiful hard worker called Nongaye. The spacious home of the Ndunganes had a large front garden and behind the house, there was a big vegetable garden. I suspect that this must have been Stanford's home.

This was to become my home for the next several months. I opened the gate and slowly walked up the sidewalk leading to a big veranda of a large house. I walked straight to a middle-aged black woman who was sitting on the veranda probably enjoying the sunlight. I greeted her and respectfully told her the story that I had been rehearsing. I said my parents could not afford to send me to school. Now I was looking for a job and intended to go back to school in the near future.

The bespectacled woman listened to my story intently and had compassion on me. She offered me a job on the spot and let me into her large house. I was given a private room and Nongaye, the domestic worker, was instructed to feed me. It was the home of the Ndunganes, and my job was going to be in the garden behind the large house.

I immediately felt like I was a part of this family. Lindelwa, the daughter who was a bit older than I, became like a sister. Mr Ndungane would arrive on Friday afternoons and leave early Monday mornings to drive back to his school near Cofimvaba. The Ndunganes were devout worshippers. We would all go to All Saints Anglican Church on Sundays where Father Ludidi would render fiery sermons.

Nongaye would always talk about him in the way that girls would talk about men when they like them. She once told Lindelwa and me that she was quite sure that Father Ludidi was not wearing trousers under his cassock!

Lindelwa almost got me into trouble once. Her boyfriend was in town from a faraway village of Mnyolo where his father was a shopkeeper. Apparently, he was in trouble for having driven his father's vehicle without permission and then smashing it. Therefore, he needed shelter for the night and appealed to Lindelwa for help. Lindelwa was not supposed to date.

In the black culture dating is forbidden, but parents are usually aware that these girl-boy relationships happen in secret and grudgingly accept that. Therefore, the parents were to be kept out of this and Lindelwa asked for help from Nongaye and another domestic helper whose name was Nobuhle, and myself.

The plan was simple. I was to move out of my room, which was on the far end of the house with relatively easy access from outside, through the window! I would sleep in the hallway and Lindelwa would collect the bedding from her room, which was just opposite her parent's one. Nongaye and Nobuhle would assist in reconfiguring the room in anticipation of the secret arrival of this important guest whose name was Sibongile.

Unfortunately for all of us, Lindelwa's parents became suspicious, as there was unusual movement in the house and probably some excitement on the part of Lindelwa!

Mr Ndungane, whom we called *Tishala* meaning teacher, decided to investigate.

He checked Lindelwa's room first and found that something was amiss, and then proceeded to Nongaye and Nobuhle's room, and then to mine. He found my bed in the hallway! "Thembinkosi, why is your bed here?" He asked fuming. I was between a rock and a hard place. On one hand, I did not want to betray Lindelwa who had become like a sister to me; but I also did not want to lie to a kind man who was like a father to me. I mumbled something and fortunately, he did not insist that I answer since *umqolo wawuphandle* - the secret was out.

Mr and Mrs Ndungane had a heated conversation with Lindelwa in the master bedroom while Nongaye, Nobuhle and I congregated in the kitchen, guilt ridden for being complicit in this plan. Eventually a somber looking Lindelwa emerged from her parent's room. The rest of the evening was unusually quiet, interrupted only by some whispers and soft giggles. I have no idea what happened to Sibongile that night and the subject never came up again.

As a 13-year-old barely in my teens, I was slowly beginning to pay attention to women! I started to feel attracted to girls. I remember a girl who attended church services with us whose name was Zimbini. I always found it difficult to take my eyes off her. I liked the way she talked, walked, and dressed. I remember one day when she was passing by the Ndungane home and it suddenly started pouring down with rain. Everyone was running for cover. Zimbini simply continued walking, composed as if nothing was happening. I thought to myself, 'this is the definition of style and class.' Unfortunately for me, I was way beneath Zimbini's standard; I could not even attempt to tell her how I felt.

Sometimes I would watch the teenage daughters of the Titus's and Nyamakazi's strolling through town looking very attractive and so unattainable! I could only watch from a distance, as I was a mere gardener.

I enjoyed my gardening job and often did things that I was never asked to do, to the great delight of Mr and Mrs Ndungane. I later learned that I was being paid double the previous employees' wages, even though I was much younger than they were.

I liked that no one told me what to do and enjoyed it very much when my work was being appreciated. While Mpendulo and the gang remained in a shack behind Wick's Supermarket hoping to find pig fat and white man's hair, I became a part of a middle-class black family in the same town.

One late Sunday morning, as I was strolling through town, I noticed some movement at the Roman Catholic Church in the road that leads to Cala. It was the end of a church service and people were leaving. The white priest was shaking the hands of the parishioners at the church door. I had never shaken the hand of a white man before and saw an opportunity to do so. It would mean a lot to me, so I thought. I quickly walked over to the church premises, joined the queue and when my turn came, I shook the hand of a white man. This was a great accomplishment for me, perhaps at some point I could find the hair as well!

When I shook that hand, little did I know that as a black South African my prospects would depend very much on my proximity to whiteness and white privilege.

When I joined the queue to shake a white man's hand, could it be that a deep inner yearning for proximity to whiteness and privilege drove me? Could it be that psychologically I was already conditioned to believe that 'white is right' and that my attitude towards whiteness would determine my altitude? Maybe it was a mere childish curiosity. I still do not know why, as a 13-year-old, I decided to join that queue to shake a white man's hand.

NELSON MANDELA IN "LONG WALK TO FREEDOM" TELLS HIS OWN STORY OF HIS INITIAL IMPRESSIONS OF WHITE PEOPLE AS FOLLOWS:

I came across a few whites as a boy in Qunu. The local magistrate, of course, was white as was the nearest shopkeeper. Occasionally a white traveler or police officer passed through our area. These whites appeared as grand as gods did to me, and I was aware that they were to be treated with a mixture of fear and respect. But their role in my life was a distant one and I thought little, if at all, about the white man in general or relations between my own people and these curious and remote figures.

Roughly about seven years later, I was to have my own experience of young children lining up to shake my hand. This happened in Perth, Western Australia when I bumped into a group of Aborigine children as I was taking a Saturday afternoon walk.

These lovely kids were having fun swimming, and as soon as they saw me, they stopped, looking at me inquisitively.

I think my blackness caught their attention just as theirs caught mine. However, we did not look quite the same, our facial features and the texture of our hair was different, but there was a connection, we were black. I went to shake their hands and to my surprise they lined up and respectfully took turns to shake my hand, "My name is Theo, and I come from Africa," I said.

"Africa!" they exclaimed as if that name rang a bell. "Yes" I said with a smile. They indicated to me with a childish innocence that they wanted to feel my hair. I bent down so they could touch it. At that moment, I recalled what my mother used to say about our hair; When we were small and she wanted us to comb it, she would make us feel that our hair was below standard, calling it "kaffir hare", kaffir being a derogatory term whites used to refer to black people and "hare" meaning hair in Afrikaans.

I was delighted when these indigenous Australian children just loved my hair. But more about my Australian experiences later.

I may have felt content and fulfilled when I shook the white man's hand at the Catholic Church in Ngcobo. However, a young man of about 14 had a different experience with a white hand. This happened inside Ngcobo town hall one Friday evening after a church service. These Friday evening services or *imvuselelos* (Revival) meetings used to take place regularly and the man behind these meetings was none other than Mr Hessel.

Mr Hessel, a tall bearded chap with a balding head, always appeared calm and collected. His command of isiXhosa was more than impressive; he could speak isiXhosa as though he was a Xhosa. Mr Hessel was a successful businessperson who owned what would be called a hypermarket today in the middle of Ngcobo along the R61, which becomes the main road. He would share stories about how he grew his business from two employees to more than 200. His employees called him *Nkosana*, which means little boss or Klein baas in Afrikaans. For some reason Mr Hessel loved to be addressed as such by his black employees. During the time of apartheid, blacks were expected to call their bosses' sons Kleinbaas.

A description of Mr Hessels would not be complete without mentioning that he was also deeply religious and gave generously to the church in its endeavors to propagate the Christian religious message. One of the perplexing things about his faith was the perpetuation of separateness in the church. Ngcobo had two church buildings of the same denomination right next to each other. One for blacks and the other for whites. Mr Hessel and a few whites who still lived in Ngcobo worshipped in the nicer building with well looked after lawns and a beautiful garden. The black church right next to it was unfenced and looked very shabby. It appeared that there was no effort to integrate these two communities of the same church.

Mr Hessel would send his trucks out to collect young people from nearby villages to attend these services. There would be singing, and people would share their stories of conversion because of the Christian message. Mr Hessel would conduct a Bible quiz and reward those who demonstrated knowledge of scriptures with sweets. A preacher would then be called to deliver a message and urge attendees to come to repentance and be born again.

The highlight for many youngsters, including myself, was always at the end of the service when Mr Hessel would reward everybody with a biscuit. It was not any biscuit; it was Lemon Creams! He would stand by the door and hand out one biscuit to each one as they exited.

On one particular Friday evening, a young chap had decided that one biscuit was not enough for him, so he decided to cheat and go for seconds. He was unaware that Mr Hessel's sharp eye missed nothing. As he was holding out his little hand to receive a biscuit for the second time Mr Hessel calmly delivered a devastating blow to his little face with an open hand. This hard clap to the face brought fear to all of us. Mr Hessel calmly said *"Uyaphinda mfana?"* (Are you coming for seconds young man!), and then just continued to hand out biscuits as if nothing happened.

I was now scared of the white hand. What if Mr Hessel mistakenly thought that I was also cheating and rendered the same grossly disproportionate punishment for my 'crime'?

Therefore, a little boy in the town of Ngcobo who was eager to shake a white man's hand soon realized that a white hand could inflict maximum pain and move on as if nothing happened. What we had considered a safe space -or even holy space - was transformed into a space of violence and fear in front of our eyes.

CHAPTER TWO

S on, I am going to train you to be an expert!" Mr Bikwana, who was known by his clan name Tshawe, said, looking very excited. "You have come to the right place and we are going to hit the road within the next hour." My new employer was unable to hide his excitement. I had gotten bored of working in the garden for the Ndunganes, even though they were so good to me and treated me with respect.

Unfortunately, my departure from their home was not a dignified one. I simply took what belonged to me and left without informing anybody and took up temporal residence next door while I looked for another job. I now understand that this was rude, and I acted childishly and displayed ingratitude to very kind people. Fortunately, the Ndunganes never seemed offended by that. Mrs Ndungane had become a friend to my mother who had become a regular visitor at the end of each month to collect a share of my stipend.

Life between the Ndunganes and the next job was not easy, but it never occurred to me that I should either go home or back to the Ndungane family.

I wanted a new experience, I prayed for a new experience. Then one afternoon a man called Bhayi met me on the street and told me that his boss was looking for a young boy who would assist him in fixing tractors and vehicles. I knew straight away that this was what I was looking for. At home I was always good at fiddling with things, from electronics (radios) to finding electrical faults in my father's old unlicensed Opel Record that used to break down frequently or simply run out of fuel. I would then have to walk several hours with a five-litre container to get petrol from the nearest filling station. We would struggle to kickstart the vehicle because the starter never worked! Once the car started, my father would continue to his destination, never bothering to drive to the filling station to fill up! I cannot recall how many trips I made to the filling station as a young boy to buy fuel. Although I must say that I really enjoyed those walks. I often proudly tell my son David about those days. I still enjoy walking to this day.

So there I was with Tshawe the mechanic. I was hired on the spot and offered accommodation, but not in a private room. I was going to be part of the family. I was going to share a room with one of his sons called Matshawe. Sometimes we slept in the lounge when there were visitors. I bonded very quickly with this family. Ntombekhaya was the eldest, then Christopher, Matshawe and Lungile. Mrs Bikwana was a schoolteacher.

Tshawe, as he was affectionately called, and I crisscrossed the region fixing tractors and sometimes motor vehicles. He was a hydraulic specialist and took pride in his work. He was a kind man and was dearly loved by his clients. He treated me with great respect and remunerated me relatively well. When my mother eventually discovered where I now worked, she was able to take more money home. Remember that there were no telephones back then, so my mother had to ask around to find me.

It was while I was working for Tshawe that I got to meet Chief George Matanzima, who was the Prime Minister of the Transkei at the time. Both KD Matanzima who was the President of Transkei and George were Tshawe's clients. We would drive to their farms in the Cofimvaba district to repair their tractors.

"Son, I don't charge them for the work we do." Tshawe once told me. "I just want them to help me get my own garage." Tshawe's efforts were rewarded because through George's assistance he was able to acquire the Shell garage in Ngcobo when the white owner left. This garage used to be known as Kwamabhovu meaning the one with a big moustache. The previous owner had an exceptionally large physique and a big moustache; apparently, he was once a feared police officer in the town.

It was while I was with this family that I first experimented with alcohol. I had been paid, and my boss was away, so I wanted to have a good time. I went to the local bottle store at Ngcobo Hotel where the white man behind the counter who had a limp allowed me to buy a bottle of Clubman even though I was under- age. I remember reading a sign on the wall, which was written in English. It read as follows, "In memory of our dear friend Credit who was brutally murdered by a gang of bad payers." At that time, my grasp of English was still poor, but I could figure out that something bad had happened to Credit and a bad gang did it. I felt sorry for the poor man.

Armed with a bottle full of Clubman I disappeared into a nearby bush behind Ulundi Hotel with a newly found friend. The wine was sweet and quite enjoyable. My new friend who was much older than me, wanted me to drink as much as possible while she only took just a couple of sips. Within minutes, I passed out and only awoke in the evening when it was already dark and my new "friend" was nowhere to be seen. My wallet was missing! I tried to find my way through the bush and eventually got home to be met by some overly concerned members of my new family.

They had been worrying about me. Apparently, I looked pathetic. They thought that I was sick or something bad had happened to me, until someone got very close to me and then shouted out "He is stone drunk!" This statement generated a lot of excitement mixed with relief and I was immediately made fun of. Ntombekhaya, or Ntosh as she was affectionately called, was a couple of years older than me and came very close to my face to make sure that I smelt of liquor. I was offended by this unwarranted attention and retaliated by using both hands to plant my long nails on both sides of Ntombekhaya's face causing her to bleed, and resulting in ugly scratches on her cheeks. Someone managed to pull me away from her and there was a lot of commotion. They eventually managed to get me to agree to go to bed.My boss Tshawe and his wife returned late that night and were promptly informed of my unbecoming behavior. I know that if there hadn't been any visible evidence, they would have kept quiet about the incident. Early the next morning Mrs Bikwana, who was Ntosh's stepmother, wasted no time. I was summoned into the bedroom and she instructed me to collect my belongings and leave at once. I expected Tshawe to intervene but he just sat there and said nothing. I walked out of the room into the hallway towards the kitchen where the rest of the family was. The atmosphere was tense, nobody was talking. I picked up my few belongings and made my way towards the door and out the gate to face an uncertain future yet again.

I walked slowly towards the town hall and then sat next to the road deep in thought. I was pondering my next move.

Interestingly, even at this stage, going back to my home in Mjanyana was not even an option. I could never go back and face Gxara, my choirmaster ever again.

I had not been sitting there for long when I heard a vehicle moving in my direction. I looked up… It was unmistakably Tshawe's Toyota Hilux, a brown utility van. While I was wondering where he was going, he suddenly halted and shouted "T'man!" The family had given me this nickname. "Jump in my boy, we have work to do." Without asking questions, I jumped into the vehicle as he drove back to the house to find a happy and relieved gang, Ntombekhaya being the happiest to see me back! She called me aside with the fresh scratches that I had caused very visible on her face. She said, "Don't worry, my mother was not angry, she was just faking it.She is just pretending that she loves me and I know she does not." Unsure as to what to say I apologized to Ntosh profusely for what I did. "Don't worry," Ntosh said looking at me with a wry smile "You were drunk *mos.*" Okay, Ntombekhaya rub it in!

Mrs Bikwana summoned me back into the big room. Of course, she had to explain why I was invited back! "The reason I changed my mind is because I remembered Madlamini's words," she explained. Madlamini is my mother's clan name. "Your mother had asked me to please look after you." I thought to myself, "My mother might have said that, but that's not the real reason. You were overwhelmingly outnumbered!' Tshawe walked in announcing that we are about to go. We both jumped into the Hilux and drove off to some distant destination to fix tractors.

My eventual exit from Tshawe's home was dignified. I had shared with him that I wanted to go back to school and his son Christopher had encouraged me to join him at Mthatha

Technical College where he was studying. Tshawe was delighted to hear that, he encouraged me to follow my heart. This was also great news for my father. My mother, however, did not show a lot of excitement, but she supported my decision.

In the later years as students of the Mthatha Technical College, we would attend the annual independence celebrations. The highlight for me was always when the soldiers made their grand entrance as they marched into the stadium. The army would sometimes do a military parade to show their might. I was so proud of our military and the fact that we were now protected and safe from white domination. I also admired the white people that stayed in the Transkei under a black government. KD had indeed set his people free without any bloodshed.

Life at Tech was good. We had several white tutors including the principal, a Mr van der Merwe who was nicknamed "Botjie" by the students. This chapter of my life was important because I was now in closer proximity with the white race. I had a student-teacher kind of relationship.

My initial observation was that there was nothing peculiar or particularly special about the white race and I was a bit disappointed that they were not as grand as my parents would have us believe. I liked Mr van der Merwe's style of leadership though. He was bearded, short in stature, muscular and walked as though he was listening to an inner rhythm. He loved his school and the students with passion.

He would make a point of walking into the dormitories and the dining hall every morning to make sure that everything was in order.

If you happened to be in the dorms during class, he would not hesitate to give you a punch or two to teach you a lesson. Even though corporal punishment was practiced in my new school, it did not amount to abuse. From my perspective as a learner there was racial harmony at the college. There were hardly any political discussions, but I do remember one morning while washing dishes in the scullery next to a senior student.

I had complained about the fact that we would sometimes be without hot water for long periods of time. On this particular morning, I wondered out loud if this was a common occurrence at the white school in town? (There were schools that still catered for whites only and I think there was some explanation for it).

My neighbour in the scullery stated that what we call independence or freedom was not really freedom. He told me that real freedom was still coming, and this was "*nomgogwana*" (imitation). He also told me that the so-called leaders of the Bantustan republics would be dealt with appropriately in due course. My schoolmate, who had a very dark complexion and a fat face, spoke hurriedly and did not give me a chance to respond. I was shattered to say the least.

CHAPTER THREE

We were sitting in a packed stadium in Mthatha, the capital of the Transkei, on a warm Sunday afternoon. It was the 25th of April 1982, a date firmly etched in my memory because it was a significant day that determined how my life would turn out.

It was the "Independence Stadium", where Transkei citizens commemorated what was called independence on an annual basis. Of course, I had attended all these events when I was a student at the technical college. I would not have known about this particular event had it not been for my newly found friends Andile Manxaile, Fuzile Fongoqa and Phathilizwe Mjali.

At Tech I had become aware of the many influences around me and I so much wanted to be a better person. I had decided to join the Student Christian Movement (SCM). I admired the few people who were part of this movement. They seemed to be unaffected by peer pressure and were not indulging in youthful desires.

This trio were members of the SCM and were zealously promoting the Christian message of rebirth and accepting Jesus Christ as lord and saviour.

I was at a stage where I was asking many questions about the meaning of life, even though I had already been introduced to religion via my early upbringing. My parents were religious and so were the Ndunganes and Bikwanas, and then there was religious instruction at primary school.

While religion never really made sense to me, what it drilled into me was a sense of guilt and a need to be forgiven and saved from a place called hell or a 'Christ less eternity', as some would say. The trio had identified me as a "seeker" who was looking for answers, hence the invitation to this event. I was told that an evangelist from Canada would be presenting a Christian message. After all the singing and praying a diminutive man who was introduced as Dr Barry Moore stood up and passionately presented a message in the form of preaching.

He spoke with such passion about the death of Jesus on the cross. I remember him explaining that the crown of thorns was buying my thoughts and the nails on his hands were buying my hands, so were the feet. "You were bought at a price!" he boomed.

At the end of his presentation he made what is called an alter call asking people to come towards the stage to make a commitment to Jesus Christ.

As he was making the call and urging people to come forward, his colleague Art Perry sang "Just as I am.

> *Just as I am, without one plea*
> *But that Thy blood was shed for me*

And that Thou bid'st me come to thee
O Lamb of God, I come, I come
Just as I am, though tossed about
With many a conflict, many a doubt
Fighting's and fears within without
O Lamb of God, I come, I come
Just as I am, poor, wretched, blind
Sight, riches, healing of the mind
Yea, all I need, in Thee to find
O Lamb of God, I come, I come

Moore was convincing and the song was just the final straw. I needed to make a decision and make it fast! I was not quite convinced that I needed to make it there and then though, but the trio had strategically placed themselves around me, and put the pressure on. It was too much! I needed to go forward, even though I was "tossed about with many a conflict, many a doubt, fighting's within, and fears without."

I stood up to the great delight of the trio and made my way to the front, joining many others who were doing the same, to the joy of Dr Barry Moore and Reverend Myeko who was the interpreter of the day. We were made to pray a 'sinner's prayer' and then a general prayer for all of us, and I became a 'Born Again' Christian.

I do not know why this decision affected me more than my three friends. My zeal surpassed that of the trio within a short period of time and I wanted desperately to be a preacher like Moore. Despite pleas from one of my instructors, I decided to abandon my studies at Tech to pursue studies in Christian theology. It was for this reason that I ended up at Kentani in what was then called the Evangeli Xhosa Bible School. However, prior to going to Bible School, I underwent a traditional Xhosa ritual of *ukoluka* which is a passage from boyhood to manhood. Circumcision is part of the ritual, it is kind of school that emphasizes the role of men in society.

Looking back, I realize that something was missing in my conversion! I became so heavenly minded and was of no earthly good. I was preoccupied with being holy and cared very little about loving my neighbour as myself. I embraced a religious lifestyle that made me think that I was better than everybody else because I was going to heaven.

In later years, I found it quite fascinating to read Wilhelm Verwoerd's testimony, the grandson of the apartheid architect Hendrik Verwoerd. This is how he describes his faith growing up as a privileged white male:

"Partly because my understanding of good and evil was strongly influenced by the puritanical culture that rippled outwards from the DRC (Dutch Reformed Church). I swallowed the long list of sins within this culture hook, line and sinker: As a dedicated Warrior for Jesus I therefore did not smoke. Alcohol was prohibited. Drugs were not an option. I tried hard not to swear or to use God's name in vain. I did not dance. Or play in my own rock band like my brothers. I didn't even listen to this "unholy" music. My anti-dance and anti-rock music sentiments were so "pure" that I had taken the lead to arrange an alternative to the Matric year-end dance: a bus to Cape Town for High Tea at the fancy Mount Nelson Hotel.

On a sadder note: Above all I diligently refrained from "inappropriate sexual activities". "Dirty thoughts" was high on my confession list during my daily Bible study and prayers. After all, good Christians strive to be "pure of heart" (Matt. 5), don't they? As a result "You may not have sex before you are married!" to me clearly was a much more important commandment than to, like the untamed Jesus, love my enemies". My blinkers as "pure" warrior for (white) Jesus was entangled with my group consciousness, with my "volksfamilie" (ethnic family). A typical entry in my English Diary during my years at Paul Roos says it all:

"I am amazed by how religion can make people think the same way irrespective of their lived experiences and unquestioningly embrace the status quo."

It turned out that I would come across Dr Moore again. This time at his offices in Canada, ten years after my conversion. I was part of a group from ten different countries that was crisscrossing America and Canada as "Missionaries to America and Canada" under the auspices of Teen Mission International, led by Bob Bland. Our team leaders were a young couple by the name of Marty and Heidi Hartley. One of the churches that had invited us was located close to London in Ontario and someone in that church happened to know Moore. I was taken to his offices to the great delight of Dr Moore.

The very last encounter I had with Moore in 1996 did not end so well. This was four years after I had met him in Canada. He had been invited to preach in the Strand near Somerset West. I attended one of his crusades at the town hall. He and Art Perry were there, almost 15 years after my conversion. I had brought my wife and stepson along to meet my hero. At that time, I had only been married for about a year, which Dr Moore knew, and my stepson was 4 years old.

Moore wanted an explanation. "Where is the father of this boy?" He asked with a stern face. I knew immediately where this was going. I had not thought of him as one of those conservative evangelicals who see divorce as an unpardonable sin. I knew that if I mentioned that Jesika had been divorced, the mood would change immediately and I was not quite prepared for that, so I tricked him a bit and said, "The father is no Moore." He immediately relaxed and the mood went back to normal. After that last encounter, I did not want to see Moore anymore.

I often wonder how my life would have turned out had I not made that decision on that day. I would have most probably qualified as a motor mechanic. I probably would have started a successful business in the motor industry. On the other hand, if I had not made that decision I would almost certainly not have had the kind of exposure to travel that I have. I have met wonderful people around the world, from all walks of life. I would have not have met the great people around me whom I consider close friends.

My life has been deeply enriched by great theologians in the Christian space. Leaders such as Dr Spiwo Xapile, a great thinker who led the JL Zwane Memorial Church for 27 years and made a huge impact in Gugulethu and indeed, throughout South Africa and Africa. Dr Deon Snyman is a good friend who led the Restitution Foundation for many years. Pastor Xola Skosana, who co-journeyed with me for many years and who is a highly gifted speaker and critical thinker. He is also the author of "The Things We Feel, Things We Dare Not Say: Disband the White Church." Dr Wilhelm Verwoerd, a humble man who is deeply bothered by the injustices of the past, and Dr Robert Steiner, who has become an important man in my life. Professor John De Gruchy also influenced me mainly through writings, and there are many others. I can identify with De Gruchy's reflections on his conversion:

Whichever way I now assess what happened, it changed the course of my life. I do not regret that for a moment, but I do regret the extent to which I was then drawn into a legalist, fundamentalist Christianity, which made me feel guilty about youth's peccadilloes, narrowed my perspective on life, and insisted on an understanding of Christian faith and the Bible that became increasingly untenable."

What excites me now is the notion of redeeming the concept of UBUNTU. I find it strange that it has not been widely linked to the teachings of Jesus. Jesus summarized the entire Bible by stating that we are to love our creator (God) deeply, love others (neighbor) deeply, as well as ourselves (as yourself). For me, Jesus is simply saying the greatest commandment is to have UBUNTU.

Then what is UBUNTU? Ubuntu has been explained in many different ways. It is probably fitting to quote the wisdom of an anonymous Zulu elder in his conversation with my white friend:

He knocked his pipe out against the stone and said to me, 'Umuntu ngumuntu ngabantu. Do you know what that means?' 'No, sir.' 'It's Zulu. It is where the word "Ubuntu" comes from. It means many things. We can only be human through other humans. We are part of a whole, of a greater group. Inextricably. The group is the individual. It means we are never alone, but it also means damage to another is damage to you. It means sympathy, respect, brotherly love, compassion and empathy.' He looked at me through his thick glasses and said, 'That is what the white man in Africa must search for. If he doesn't find it, he will forever be a stranger in this land.'

— BLOOD SAFARI, DEON MEYER

I think authentic Christlikeness is to embrace the spirit of UBUNTU. It is to seek justice and 'to do unto others what you would have them do unto you'.

I would like to see myself as a Christian who firmly embraces the African notion of UBUNTU, an "Ubuntuist or a Christian humanist who strives to reach higher levels of emotional and spiritual intelligence (EQ &SQ).

Because, "when emotional intelligence merges with spiritual intelligence, human nature is transformed."- Deepak Chopra.

CHAPTER FOUR

"Sir, have you identified your luggage?" "No" I responded. "Then identify your luggage and move to the other side." The Zimbabwean custom official shouted impatiently and looked irritated. I could not help noticing that he was not as friendly with me as he was with the Australian passengers at the Harare International Airport.

In southern Africa it is not uncommon to see black people bending over backwards, smiling and being extra friendly when dealing with white people, and then those same people demonstrating a different attitude to those of their own race. I sometimes watch cashiers with amusement in shopping malls being super nice to the white clients and not as nice to fellow blacks. I guess one can argue and say that it is all superficial. It is part of the survival mode that is deeply ingrained in the African people.

I was in Harare on my way to Perth in Western Australia. I had to fly via Zimbabwe as there were no direct flights from South Africa because of sanctions imposed by the international community. I had now learnt that being a Transkeian could not get you far, literally! I could not travel anywhere with a Transkei passport, I had to get a South African one and become a South African citizen again.

I was going to Australia to do training with an international organization called YWAM (Youth with a Mission). My mission in life had now changed. Fixing engines had become secondary and sharing my faith with the world had become my primary goal. I had just finished my four-year Theological training in Kentane, and a former lecturer and friend Timothy Mitchell and his wife Pauline had helped to raise funds for my airfare to Australia. I was promised assistance on the other side of the Indian Ocean.

Centane, also known as Kentane, is located about 26 km east of Butterworth, and its only claim to fame is that is the site of the last frontier war that the Amaxhosa fought with the white settlers on the 7th of February 1878 where the Amaxhosa were defeated. The nine frontier wars were fought over a 100-year period.

Reverend H Oosthyzen and his wife Mrs G Oosthyzen opened a Bible college not far from the battle site. Ironically, the type of theology they taught was about the battle that Christians ought to fight with the evil one. The evangelistic outreaches that we did were called campaigns. The training itself was done in a semi-military fashion. The focus was not on academic achievement but on character development, and Oosthyzen's favorite subject was Practical Theology.

As the QANTAS aircraft cruised comfortably at nearly 1000 km an hour, I was conscious of the fact that I was going to a white world and wondering what the future held. I initiated a conversation with my neighbor who was a young Australian man. I do not remember what we spoke of, only that he lost interest when I tried to convert him.

I had been taught to use every opportunity to introduce people to Christ and here I was with someone sitting next to me for ten hours, a captive audience so to speak. When he lost interest, I felt that I had done my duty, I had shown the sinner the error of his ways, and therefore his blood was not on my hands. I then started to think about other things. I thought of the people that I was leaving behind.

I thought of all the fund raising that was done to make this trip a reality. I thought of Timothy and Pauline's efforts as they did everything in their power to raise the airfare. Timothy and I made beds and tried to sell them, Pauline made chicken curry and sold it at the Butterworth bus rank; she was the only white face there.

I thought of Dr Justin Mitchell (Timothy's father) who was retired but would put on his suit and drive to the Australian embassy from his Pretoria home to try to get my visa. He did this several times. I thought of Mrs Mitchell's delicious meals enjoyed during my short stay at their lovely home in Pretoria while waiting for my visa. I thought of the jacaranda trees that line up the streets of South Africa's administrative capital.

I thought of the exhilarating feeling I had as I experienced my first flight ever. I thought of my family back at Gotyubeni. I thought of my childhood days when we used to shout at passing aircrafts that occasionally invaded our air space *"Undiphatheliswiti!"* (You must bring back sweets!) I wondered if the children of Zimbabwe and Mozambique had shouted at this very aircraft with the same requests. I thought of aircrafts that go down and disappear into the sea. I then offered a silent prayer for our aircraft. After my prayer I thought about many other things, some important and some not so important until I fell asleep.

I was awoken by a commotion. The aircraft was shaking violently. I was quite convinced that it was the end of us. The "sinner" that was seated next to me was not showing any fear. I had shared with him earlier that Christians do not fear death. I realized that I was wrong; maybe I should have said 'they are not *supposed* to fear death'.

I pretended not to be scared, put on a brave face and smiled. Later I learned that this occurrence is called turbulence and is not uncommon when flying in bad weather.

Later the pilot apologized even though it was not his fault. So, the next time we hit an air pocket I was not as scared. Besides those two glitches, the flight was uneventful and quite enjoyable. We touched down in Perth, Western Australia, just after ten in the morning. It had been a long flight, and I was quite apprehensive.

We lined up as we went through customs. The customs officials scanned the documents and stamped and let people through. It seemed to me that it was just a simple exercise. But then it was my turn at the counter. The simple scanning was not enough, it turned into an inspection. After the customs agent satisfied himself that everything was in order, he asked, "Is there anything to declare?" to which I responded "No".

"Do you have anything edible in your baggage?"

"No Sir," I answered.

"Do you know what edible means?" He asked rather demandingly.

"Yes."

"What does it mean?" He demanded to know.

"Something that you can put in your mouth and eat, sir!" I said timidly. He motioned me to move on. Little did I know that scrutiny by customs officials would follow me all the days of my life!

My Australian experience was the first of many. I can tell you similar or worse stories about my experiences in the UK, Germany, Sweden and the USA. I was once interrogated at J F Kennedy Airport in the US for almost an hour. My suspicion that I was being singled out because of my skin colour was confirmed by a phone-in programme I listened to on the radio about the unfair treatment of blacks by customs officials in Europe.

"The UK deported me because I'm black, says SA woman." This is the story of a certain Amanda Phali from Port Elizabeth who was detained at London's Gatwick Airport, grilled, photographed, fingerprinted, and deported. "In a letter to Phali" the article continues," the immigration service was not 'satisfied that you are genuinely seeking entry as a visitor for the limited period stated by you'. It speculated that Phali might have been brought to the UK to work as a nanny for the Allen's" (the sponsors).

"I was treated like a prisoner, locked for 10 hours in a room with no window," Phali claims. I must admit that I have never been subjected to treatment as extreme. By the way, my own sister Kholeka saved up to visit the UK and never went further that the airport for the same reasons.

I once listened to a person giving a spiritual analysis of the UK and some positive developments there. He summarized his statement by saying "the UK is OK". Maybe for black visitors the UK is not OK.

As I stepped out of the airport building, I was welcomed by an intense heat wave, the temperature must have been hovering at around 35 degrees C, and it was late January. I had always thought that Africa was the hottest place in the world. At the airport, a kind man called Patrick from the YWAM base in Hay Street picked me up. I cannot recall a single thing that Patrick and I talked about as we drove to the base; I can only remember what he was wearing, which is so unlike me. I always remember what people said and not what they wore.

The base looked deserted; the students were out for the day and would be coming back to the base after having what Patrick called a barbeque. I later learned that a barbeque is just another word for what we call a braai. The moment I was shown my bed I just collapsed on it and soon I was fast asleep. I was so thankful that there was no one around so I could rest peacefully.

I woke up when the students got back and immediately began to feel very conspicuous when I realized that I was the only black person around. I came from a country that was majority black and had never really felt outnumbered. Now here I was, in Australia with just the white race, having to deal with the inferiority complex that my parents had helped to instill in my mind. It won't be long before my intellectual shortcomings are exposed, I thought. But the students were very nice to me.

They wanted me to feel welcome. They asked questions about apartheid South Africa. I told them that I was not really a South African, that I was a Transkeian. They wanted to know what the difference was between the two states. I told them that Transkei was a free country. I told them that my country was now under the military dictatorship of a chap called General Bantu Holomisa. The students asked me many other questions and I tried to answer them all. I soon began to settle and was liked by students and staff.

My inferiority complex soon dissipated. I felt loved and accepted. I attended some of the bicentennial celebrations that were held in the city. Australia was turning two hundred ,although I had seen some posters declaring that 'Australia has a Black history.'

I liked Australia. I also asked many questions, I wanted to know about the Aborigines. I discovered that it was a subject that people would rather avoid, except to say that they are a lazy bunch that abuse Australia's welfare system by their refusal to work and their habit of excessive alcohol consumption.

I did not feel that there was any appreciation of their history and their pain. I began to feel that this black race of Australia was treated by the white race exactly the way I was treated at home. I felt that as an outsider though, I was highly regarded. Many ex-South Africans invited me into their homes.

They would tell me that they left South Africa because of apartheid. I must say that it was quite strange for me to hear whites from South Africa condemning apartheid. In all my interaction with whites in South Africa, there had never been any condemnation of apartheid. Whites simply enjoyed their privileged status and related to the blacks at their level. I travelled around Australia and never felt once that I was being discriminated against because of my race. In South Africa, you subconsciously knew that whites did not like you until they proved otherwise.

There was a constant struggle for acceptance at home; here in Australia it was different, so I thought. The more I stayed in Australia the more I began to question my understanding of politics. I realized how ignorant I was.

People would ask me what I thought of Archbishop Desmond Tutu. I would simply echo what the South African government said: 'A clergy turned politician'. One day I walked into what was called "People's Library" in Perth and saw a book on the shelf entitled "South Africa's Transkei". I read the book, which greatly enhanced my political knowledge. I began to question many of the things that KD said when he addressed us at my very first political rally.

I also went to watch to Richard Attenborough's movie Cry Freedom, about Steve Biko and Donald Wood. which deeply moved me.

I gradually began to see myself not as a Transkeian but as a South African whose citizenship has been denied. I recalled the things that the man with a fat face had told me in the scullery years back. I questioned the origins of the rumors of war in our quiet village of Gotyubeni. The truth began to emerge, and little bits of the puzzle were coming together. I was beginning to understand many things.

I then discovered that when the South African government introduced the Bantu Authorities Act in the 1950s, the Bunga, the council of Transkei chiefs, rejected it. Matanzima, however, persuaded the Bunga to accept the Act in 1955. The Act was intended by South Africa to give chiefs more local power, but at the same time use them as puppets to control the homelands. In 1963, the South African authorities granted Transkei self-government, and Matanzima was elected as chief minister. Soon afterwards, he founded the Transkeian National Independence Party with his brother, George Matanzima.

Kaiser Matanzima started pressing the South African government for independence, and in 1976 Transkei was the first Black homeland to become independent, with Matanzima as Prime Minister. His brother George became the Minister of

Justice. But it was independence in name only the Transkei remained reliant on finances and military aid from South Africa, and apart from Israel and Taiwan, no other foreign country would accept its sovereignty.

Enough of the homeland politics for now. My desire was to meet the Australian Aborigines, to hear them speak about life in Australia as a black person. I had heard that some of them wanted a separate homeland for themselves and that the government was open to the idea of giving them the remotest state called the Northern Territory. I wanted to hear their story. A friend of mine, Kathy Wilson, took me to an Aboriginal project one day.

They seemed delighted to see me and were keen to talk, on condition that I would come alone. Kathy seemed bothered by the fact that her presence was not required. I, on the other hand, was pleased that this black race on the other side of the Indian Ocean wanted to share its secrets with a fellow black man from Africa. I told Kathy it was OK, I would simply return on a different day on my own.

I did return on my own and a bigger meeting was set where I would meet some Aboriginal elders. I was also expected to address them. They were keen to hear more about Africa and South Africa in particular. This was going to be my first political presentation ever. I was already a preacher, so I had done many gospel presentations before, but this was different.

I was not on my own, I was accompanied by a friend whose name was Bridget Precious. Bridget was an ex-Rhodesian. That is another thing about Australia; almost everybody I met was an 'ex-something'. Bridget was a white middle-aged woman with long greyish hair; she looked like she had been exceptionally beautiful when she was younger. Bridget lived through a difficult time in her homeland country of Rhodesia, now Zimbabwe, during the bush war. She had many horrifying stories to tell.

She once told me that she came across nine corpses of family and friends at different times during the war, how that affected her health and how she left Zimbabwe with nothing. She lived on her own in a flat and her passion was Africa. Bridget would collect second-hand clothing from her church community and send them to communities in Africa. This lady became like a mother to me and supported me through very difficult emotional times.

I must have said something about Bridget to my Aboriginal friends that got her accepted. The meeting was informal and was preceded by a barbeque, after which I was given an opportunity to do a presentation. I had done my best to prepare my speech. My main source was Patrick Johnson's "Operation World", as well as information gathered from newspapers. My mind at this stage was quite engrossed in politics; I felt that something was missing in my understanding of the political landscape.

The year was 1988 and I was 22 years old. These are some snippets of the speech:

ECONOMY

South Africa is the richest and most industrialized country in Africa. It is the world's biggest exporter of non-petroleum minerals-especially gold, platinum chrome, diamonds and coal. Lack of water and erratic rainfall could limit growth. World recession, drought and worldwide opposition to the racial policies have further stimulated government overspending on the cumbersome administration of separate development and defense.

That is what apartheid is it is separate development or segregation. Inflation and severe decline in the economy since 1982 have been the consequence. Whites earn on average three times as much as Blacks.

POLITICS

The union of South Africa was formed in 1910. A white parliamentary republic was created in 1961. The exclusion of blacks from national politics and the compartmentalization of the races are the major unresolved issues which dominate every aspect of national life. Government policy continues to be:

One: to work toward independent Black states for each of the ten ethnic groups.

Two: to gradually dismantle the structures of discriminatory apartheid.

Three: to form a constellation of ethnic states economically linked together.

Changes are coming, but too fast for the fearful whites and far too slow for the frustrated blacks.

Now let us come to the whole subject of economic sanctions. Since 1946 the United Nations has been trying to bring about peaceful change in South Africa. It has helped mobilize world opinion and action against apartheid. In view of the apartheid regime's intransigence, it has now imposed mandatory, but only partial sanctions on South Africa in the form of arms embargo and has called for wider sanctions on a voluntary basis.

An overwhelming majority of the state members of the United Nations are convinced that further sanctions against the Pretoria regime, particularly comprehensive and mandatory sanctions, have become imperative and that such sanctions constitute peaceful means to eliminating apartheid. They believe that sanctions have an effect and that the apartheid regime is vulnerable to international action is a general opinion. There is, therefore, a strong case for more effective sanctions against South Africa, in the interest of accelerating the process of the elimination of apartheid and minimizing the violence and bloodshed.

This is an illustration of the consequences of economic sanctions. The rand (SA currency is in rands), which was worth some USD 0.53 last year (compared to nearly USD 0.90 in early '84), plummeted following the uncompromising speech made by President Botha in Durban.

When it dipped below US 0.37 the following month, the Reserve Bank closed the foreign exchange market. The rand is now being closely monitored and in Dec '85, the Reserve Bank established exchange controls and separated the commercial rand from the financial rand. The commercial exchange rate for the rand has now climbed back to around US 0.49. Prices are climbing rapidly while the wages are fluctuating. Some people in the black community say the reaction is less violent; there is just another drop of misery in an ocean of tragedy. I will let you judge for yourself.

Australia is one of the leading countries on sanctions against South Africa. Now the question is: do pressures from outside help South African society to evolve, or are they counter-productive? Much has been written on this subject to which there is no simple answer.

I have consciously left out the embarrassing part of my speech where I stunned my audience by lambasting them for their poor state of affairs and gave them quite a large overdose of Christianity. I quoted scriptures and suggested that they should become missionaries, and all would be well.

Now with the benefit of hindsight I can see how judgmental, insensitive, and immature I was. I sometimes wish I could go back to that group, apologize, and give them a revised speech. I must mention that the Aboriginal people of Australia still have a special place in my heart. I recall two other encounters with Aboriginal communities.

My other encounter was when I once walked past a pub in Hay Street, and a group of Aborigines came running towards me and shouted "Brother! Where are you from?" I noticed that they had had a few drinks, but that did not really matter, they were my brothers! There was what I call social affinity. The black connection. "I am from Africa". I responded. "Africa!" They exclaimed just as the children had with a sense of identification.

Then these original inhabitants surprised me by emptying their pockets of all the coins they had and stuffed them into my pockets. The cash came in handy, as I was dire need at the time. That really touched me.

You might have noticed that in my speech there was no mention of Transkei. In my mind, Transkei had ceased to be a political entity. It had become quite clear to me that the "independence" of Transkei was Pretoria's orchestration.

Once my mind had been cleared of the political confusion, I began to enjoy Perth. I would take long walks across the city. I particularly enjoyed window shopping at the Hay Street Mall. On Saturdays, I would ride a bicycle along the Swan River on those nice pushbike paths. Initially it was a bit strange to see old people, and mothers with babies also riding bicycles. Once I tried to ride to Freemantle but realized that I was not fit enough! Peter Brownhill, a red-bearded fellow whom I had initially met in the Transkei while on a mission's trip, was our base leader. Everything was communicated through Timothy, my white missionary friend and lecturer, and even after I arrived in Australia, there was very little communication between Peter and myself. I do not doubt that he and Shirley, his wife, cared for me, but I was bothered by a nagging feeling that I was some kind of project, a black project, an African project?

The feeling I had was aggravated or rather, justified, when I became emotionally involved with Kathy Wilson, the white Australian lady who first introduced me to the Aboriginal community. I had just finished my training and all my classmates had returned to their respective homes. I was to stay at the base for a longer period. Kathy had finished her training months earlier and had returned to the base to help while contemplating her next move.

The two of us became close and before we knew it, we were romantically attached. We communicated this to the person in charge, Patrick (the same person that had picked me up the airport), as Peter was away on yet another mission's trip. Patrick told us that he had no authority to give the relationship the 'go ahead', even though he did not think it would be a problem.

You see, our base had rules, no, there were not rules I remember Patrick once explained. They were principles; he did explain the difference between the two, but I cannot remember.

According to the principles, one could not have a romantic relationship without special permission from the base leader. Another important principle was that even if permission was granted, there was to be "no physical contact".

So, Kathy and I had never held hands or kissed or any of that stuff, we just knew that we liked each other very much, we enjoyed each other's company and we were simply asking the leadership to endorse our growing relationship. What we were asking was something that dozens of others had asked for before, and Patrick did not think that it was going to be a problem. Kathy and I did not think so either.

We were all wrong! To Peter it was a problem. No reason was stated except that it would divert my focus from the main reason why I was invited. Up until then I did not really know what the main reason for my invitation was, it had never been communicated. I cried in front of Peter begging for an explanation and asking for Kathy and me to be allowed to enjoy each other's company.

All my pleas and cries fell on deaf ears. This was probably the most traumatic time of my life. Kathy and I met to talk and tried to figure out what the real problem was. Kathy thought *she* was the problem, she thought that Peter did not think she met my standard.

I never told Kathy what I thought, but I certainly did not think she was the problem. I was convinced it had a lot to do with the fact that I was a black African. Kathy and I were in this kind of dilemma for many days. How does one handle this? Do you just tell your emotions to go? How do you detach yourself from someone you love? Do you just shift gears and move on as if nothing happened?

Then one day Kathy told me that Peter wanted to see her. We hoped that perhaps he had changed his mind and that we would be allowed to go out. I remember looking at her as she walked towards Peter's house hoping that she would come back with good news. Ten or fifteen minutes later, she came back looking serious. I immediately sensed that she was not bringing back good news. "How did it go Kathy?" I asked anxiously.

Her reply stunned me. She blamed me for dragging her into a relationship and said that I had exploited her weakness and God was never in this relationship.

Kathy was a deeply spiritual person, she had told me several times that she was in peace about our relationship, and she had shared a number of scriptures that God had given her. So, when she mentioned God I cut in and said "But Kathy, did you not give scriptures that…" Kathy told me she did not want to discuss this with me and then walked away. Black man, you are alone, so I thought. This is all the Black man's fault.

I then began to wonder what the meeting between Peter and Kathy was about. The pain I was feeling at that time was unbearable. I cried many tears. I felt a deep sense of betrayal. It was difficult to face each new day.

Kathy treated me as if I was a stranger. I would pretend that all was ok while I was dying inside. I had no friends to talk to. I remember crying again in Peter's living room and Peter said sympathetically, "God is putting steel into your emotions."

I got to a point where I could not take it anymore.

I took a drug overdose. I did not really want to die, I just wanted another kind of pain. I thought physical pain would be more tolerable than emotional pain. I ended up in hospital where a pipe was pushed down my throat to drain the poison out of my system.

I enjoyed my brief stay at the hospital away from Kathy and away from Peter. Here I was getting a lot of attention, the doctors and nurses were all very friendly, and my situation was monitored right throughout the night.

I was also greatly encouraged when some of my former classmates came to see me when they heard what had happened. The students had a rapport with each other, my very special friends were Erin Mc Namara (Aus.), John Perkins (USA), Marcus Haussler (Swiz) and Phil Melsopp (NZ) who was a staff member.

On my return to South Africa, Peter handed me a letter to give to Timothy. I suspected that the letter was about the "real" purpose for which I was invited to Australia. I then broke my own principles and opened a letter that was not addressed to me. I convinced myself that there was a compelling reason to do this. Perhaps my curiosity was that compelling reason.

The letter was a sort of report to Timothy about my behavior while in Australia. It was a positive and paternalistic letter that also explained a "little issue about our African brother and Australian girl". I promptly destroyed the letter. My pain was a little issue!

As for Kathy, I think she was young and naïve. I found it interesting though, that she never wanted to explain the reason for her sudden change of mind.

The whole saga felt like a terrible betrayal, although I am not bitter about the fact that things never worked out between us. It simply was never meant to be. I do not want to give the impression that Australia was a big bad experience.

Years later I met a lovely woman that I dated for two years before we got married. She had been married before and had a child, as mentioned in an earlier chapter. This turned out to be a challenge for me as some of my Christian friends were very convinced that divorce is a sin.

The Christian community is deeply divided around the question of divorce. There are some who believe that a divorce should only happen when there has been marital unfaithfulness. If it does happen, one cannot remarry, as that would be adultery. In other words, one cannot marry a divorcee. Divorced individuals often experience stigmatization in many Christian communities.

Jesika and I had been married for eighteen years when we got divorced. You often hear divorced couples say that their marriage was made in hell. I certainly cannot say that about mine. During our marriage, we worked in Khayelitsha and lived in Langa - a huge adjustment for someone like her who was classified coloured (mixed race) and had been raised in a coloured neighborhood. We were able to travel to different parts of the world. We also raised two wonderful boys who are now men.

From my point of view, hell would have been a very small part of it. Jesika and I divorced as friends when our journey reached a *cul de sac*. Our attorney must have been quite surprised to see us chatting and laughing when we went to sign the divorce papers! Having said that, divorce is still a very painful experience.

After divorce, your wheels literally come off and you must start life all over again. It is even more difficult if you are regarded as a Christian leader and your colleagues simply do not know how to relate to you. I had some experiences where Christian leaders who would normally be honored to have me in their church, would now not even acknowledge my presence.

My mourning turned into dancing again when I met Gabisile "Thandeka" Sithole. My sister Thandiswa gave Gabisile her second name.

We had a private traditional wedding in the Eastern Cape and then Reverend Dr Robert Steiner formalized it at Rondebosch United with our friends Nokubonga Mepeni and Deon Snyman as our witnesses. This happened when I was serving as an associate minister at JL Zwane Presbyterian Church in Gugulethu. One of my highlights in Australia was when our team participated at World Expo '88 in Brisbane as hosts and hostesses. We were at the Pavilion of Promise, a Christian pavilion that featured a very hi-tech presentation of the Gospel. Thousands went through the Pavilion of Promise every day.

We had opportunities to visit other pavilions as well. To my disappointment Kenya was the only country that represented Africa, and while other countries put their best foot forward, the lone African pavilion seemed to be running on a shoestring budget.

I was surprised to find that most people in the West, including Australia, think that Africa is just one nation. To illustrate this point, one day I was informed that "my" Prime Minister would be visiting the Christian pavilion and I was to be his personal escort. "Even though you live in Australia now he is still your Prime Minister," the man said. It turned out that this was some government minister from Kenya who never even pitched.

I was impressed by the technological display at the Japanese Pavilion. I remember that the pavilion that represented the Vatican had an extraordinary display of affluence. The 21 days that I spent as host at World Expo'88 in Brisbane got me to see a glimpse of innovation in many countries.

My time in Australia was rapidly coming to an end. It had been a learning curve. I could not wait to return to Mother Africa where I could again blend with the crowds and be myself. I said good-bye to all my new-found friends and boarded the Qantas aircraft to take me back to my land.

I do not recall my thoughts as I headed home. I do remember the uneasy feeling that I had been a project that had gone horribly wrong.

I was excited and glad to finally return home.

We touched down at Harare airport in the early afternoon. I was struck by the contrast in relation to the airport in Perth where the airport building was air-conditioned, everything was computerised and the queues moved swiftly. The Harare airport was just the opposite. That did not matter that much to me, I was in Africa and felt at home.

I experienced a bit of reverse culture shock as we travelled in the shuttle bus from the airport to the city. I was seated next to a black Zimbabwean woman; I became aware that her husband was seated three rows behind us.

My immediate reaction was to vacate my seat and kindly invite the man to sit next to his wife. My fellow African brother interpreted my kind gesture differently. He made it quite clear, in an unkind manner, that he had no intention to sit next to his wife and where he was seated was none of my business. His male companion nodded in agreement.

I sheepishly returned to my seat next to a hugely embarrassed woman. I took comfort by reminding myself that I was now in Africa. Africans do things differently. I strongly suspect though that if a white person had made a similar gesture my fellow African friend would have either obliged or politely turned down the offer. I think the black readers will understand why I make that assumption. This is what Chika Onyeni, the author of Capitalist Nigger, cannot understand about the Black race.

He states, "From the time the Caucasians came to Africa in the 1600s till now, we are always the group to offer hospitality to our conquerors. Moreover, even at this late hour, we seem to lack the intelligence necessary to examine the ramifications of our actions since then. We are rooted to our victim instinct, accept the oppressor in your midst, make him extremely comfortable, give him all your respect and all your possessions, disrespect of your women, but then turn around to complain about his unfairness."

However, I was quite impressed by the woman who helped carry my bags to the taxi that would take me to the YWAM base in Harare. This kind woman even politely turned down my generous tip. The taxi driver was equally friendly. The folks at the YWAM base in Harare were expecting me and were extremely hospitable, although I was a bit surprised to find that all the personnel were white. I had expected the Zimbabwe base to be unlike South Africa, one that included black staff. My initial impressions of Harare as a city were good. It was tidy and bustling with friendly people.

Zimbabweans had such good relations with the world while South Africans were seen as the skunks of the world. Zimbabwe was then the food basket of Africa. President Mugabe was hailed worldwide as one of a new breed of African leaders.

A white Zimbabwean woman had this to say about President Mugabe:

> One thing I feared the most was a Mugabe government, but after independence one thing I fear the most is a government without Mugabe leading it.

That was back in 1988 and the Zimbabwe back then is not the Zimbabwe of Today. It would be interesting to come up with an accurate chronological account of events that have led to the current economic meltdown for the benefit of South Africans in particular.

I was flying Air Zimbabwe from Harare to Johannesburg. While waiting at the airport I found myself wondering whether the pilots would be black or white. I knew down deep in my heart that if I were to make a choice, I would choose white pilots, and I was bothered by the fact that I felt that way. I realized that I was a product of apartheid and had been born into a world where white was right.

I am ashamed to admit that as we walked towards the aircraft, I caught a glimpse of the two pilots in the cockpit, and the fact that they were white gave me great relief.

As we were approaching Johannesburg, an Indian woman seated next to me commented that one could feel the tension in the air now that we were entering an apartheid domain. I am not sure if I was feeling anything.

I think all I wanted was to get out of that plane and blend with the crowds. I had been feeling conspicuous for an entire year, and now I was going to look like everybody else, and I would be able to speak my native language again. One of the things I remember doing when I went into the city was buying a packet of fish and chips and sitting on the pavement to enjoy it. For the first time in my life it felt good to be black among the blacks. I just looked like everybody else.

While in Pretoria, Timothy drove me to Delmas in the then Eastern Transvaal to a meeting at the YWAM base there. We were going to explore the possibility of me joining YWAM South Africa; I was open to that possibility. When we arrived at this old mining town turned YWAM base the place just repelled me for some reason. I could never imagine myself staying in a place like that. It was suffocating. When we met with the leadership, which was all white, to explore the possibility of me joining them, my mind was already made up. That chapter closed as soon as it opened.

The first thing I did when I got back to the Transkei was to visit my homestead at Gotyubeni. As we approached home, I noticed for the first time the beauty of the Nkobongo Mountain that is peering over my village. "This mountain is beautiful" I commented softly to the driver who was from the same area and had kindly given me a lift. He gave me a blank look. I immediately knew that I should have kept the comment to myself!

People at home were delighted to see me, but I think they were a bit disappointed that I was still as poor. Rural communities believe that if you go to the cities or overseas you must always come back better off. After spending a few days with my folks, I went back to a little town called Idutywa situated between East London and Mthatha.

Here I stayed with friends for a while and people noticed that I was a little different. I did not like to dress up formally for church as everybody else seemed to. Australia had transformed me into an informal dresser! I also found that the fact that I had travelled had somewhat elevated my status in some circles, and people were trying hard to put up with my rather un-African behaviour.

CHAPTER FIVE

The beautiful Helderberg basin consists of three towns namely, Gordon's Bay, flanked by the Indian Ocean and the Helderberg mountains, which are also known as the Hottentots Holland. Then there is the Strand on the beachfront, characterized by multi-storey blocks of flats all along the beach, a holidaymaker's paradise for the privileged. The biggest of the three towns is Somerset West, which boasts enormous mansion-like houses on its hills. This town, which is reputed to have the highest number of millionaires in Africa per capita, is situated at about 45km from the city Cape Town.

It is also here in the old *Moeder Kerk* in the centre of town where church segregation is alleged to have started. The three towns are a classic example of race-based inequalities

So, you have a situation where there are lily-white churches that are relatively well off, coloured churches that are barely managing and black churches that are not managing at all. This is common in South Africa.

It was in this context that Somerset West Baptist Church saw the need to hire a black preacher who would work in a nearby black township called Lwandle. Lwandle was, in fact, not a township; it was a block of hostels where literally hundreds of families lived in poverty and unhygienic conditions, a place where one could hardly hope to raise a normal family.

The minister of the Baptist church, Dave Sayer, had called me and invited me to meet with the leadership of the church in a meeting scheduled for Monday the 12th of February 1990. My arrival in Cape Town on the 11th February coincided with another great event that had captured the attention of the world. This was the day when Nelson Mandela was released from jail after 27 years. I have a vivid recollection of the television footage as I watched this event unfold before my very eyes. It was a day that black people thought would never come. I was overwhelmed as my emotions welled up within me, trying hard to hold back the tears. This was the time when one realized that the winds of change "were unstoppable. Freedom was indeed coming.

The leadership of the church had agreed to appoint me as a Religious Practitioner whose main aim would be to convert the community. I would be accommodated in a small hut amid the hostels. I later learned that this church was one of the richest in the basin.

It was during my time in Lwandle that I met an elderly man by the name of Mr Rasmeni, who would visit me almost every day to find out how I was doing. Mr Rasmeni, who I respectfully addressed as Tata *(father)*, was a lay preacher who had worked in the Strand for many years.

Tata would tell me sad stories of humiliation, exploitation, assault and sometimes detention. He would talk about the burden of being black. He recalled that whenever he had his annual leave; the young white bosses would ask mischievously, "Are you going home to make another baby?" He would give the expected response. The young chaps would then kill themselves with laughter. "You dare not offend them," Tata would say. "Give them the answer they want and you will be ok". This information was of course not new to me. This was the rule that my own father lived by. It was a survival tactic.

Tata Rasmeni once warned me about the coloured people. "You must be very careful when you walk alone because they see us (blacks) as soft targets". I gradually became aware of the serious tensions that existed under the cool surface between the black and coloured communities, particularly in the Cape.

This is definitely the result of the racial hierarchy instituted by both colonial and apartheid administrations in order to divide and rule. I have heard people claim that coloured people are the racist people in South Africa. This is incorrect. I argue that coloured and black people cannot be racist. According to Robin Diangelo, the author of WHITE FRAGILITY, to understand racism, we need to first distinguish from mere prejudice and discrimination. All humans have prejudice and we cannot avoid it. However,' racism is a structure, not an event Diangelo correctly points out.

Coloured people may hold prejudices and discriminate against black people, but they lack the social and institutional power that transforms their prejudice and discrimination into racism. The impact of their prejudice on blacks or even whites is temporal and contextual.

However, there was a time in South Africa when an unofficial attempt was made by high profile individuals to reclassify the coloureds as blacks, but the idea never gained any traction. I have always sensed that some coloured people reject blackness and embrace brownness instead. I suppose brown is better than black. I however, ended up making friends with many coloured people and found them quite pleasant. I obviously never took Tata's warning seriously because I ended up marring a very beautiful coloured girl.

I think it is important for coloured and black people to start having conversations around prejudice in their quest to end structural racism.

Life at Lwandle hostel was lonely and tough. Misery was written in the faces of nearly everybody. Alcohol consumption was a major problem, and assault and murders were common. Sometimes up to nine families would be sharing a room with their children. Yes, I could share some Good News with them that when they die, they would go to heaven, but I was not addressing their present plight. I would go through bouts of depression. Sometimes I wondered if I was perhaps too spiritual and of no earthly good?

There were a few people from the white church that made life a little more bearable for me. While in Lwandle I met a special person whose name was Marge Constance. Marge was a pensioner and advanced in years. Her husband Harvey was sickly and needed a lot of attention, yet Marge would frequently make time to drive to Lwandle and try to make a difference. Her role was to just be with the poor, listen, and do whatever she could. She was the white mother of Lwandle and loved by everybody.

CHAPTER SIX

My tenure in Lwandle was only one year. I was overwhelmed by the challenges of the hostel dwellers and did not think that my continued presence there would really make a difference. I returned to the Transkei at the beginning of 1991. Soon after that I was asked to join a team of young people that would travel around South Africa to preach and promote the ministry of Teen Missions International. It was during that time that I was asked if I would consider becoming a South African representative of young missionaries from across the globe that would travel around America and Canada for a year. I was asked to pray about this invitation and come back with an answer from the Lord.

I honestly did not see the need to pray about the opportunity to travel and see the world. I had already been to Australia and thought it would be great to see other countries too. I immediately told the TMI organizers that I was in. This was an answer to my prayer.

They seemed a bit surprised that I would respond so promptly and admitted that it was the first time that someone accepted the invitation without prayer. I will not talk about my many experiences in both the United States and Canada over a period of 12 months of travelling almost nonstop crisscrossing America and Canada as "Missionaries to America". This would require another book.

It was while I was in America that I reconnected with Somerset West through correspondence. Pastor Kobus Swartz, whom I had met when I was working in Lwandle, had sent a letter to my home in the Transkei and my friends redirected it to America where I was. The letter was inviting me to come and work with him in Somerset West. Kobus, a white man, led a church made up of mostly coloured people, with just a few white people. After a few months at this church, I gathered that my role was to bring black people from Lwandle where I once ran a church.

Kobus so desperately wanted his church to be multiracial. I found myself in a rather awkward situation because we never had open conversations about the need for this church to be multiracial.

I was not opposed to the idea, but I needed the rationale. It would be important to note that at this time, Mandela had been released from prison and we were approaching the dawn of a new political dispensation. Democratic elections were about to be realized for the first time. Many white people wanted to be relevant and distance themselves from what would be called 'apartheid churches'.

But they still wanted to lead and were never transparent enough or made attempts to build relationships based on trust. My tenure at Hottentots Holland Community church was short lived. The name was later changed to Bizweni.

I really did not want to spend my time and energy in a 'white project' and being treated as a project myself. I wanted to reach out to young people in the most disadvantaged areas of Cape Town. It was after a short visit to Khayelitsha Township that I realized that that is where I wanted to be. Khayelitsha is a partially informal township in the Western Cape, South Africa, on the Cape Flats in Cape Town. The name is Xhosa for *Our New Home*. It is reputed to be the largest and fastest-growing township in South Africa and has a population of about half a million.

It was in this Black township that I started to visit young people who were unchurched. I invited them to a youth-friendly church called "The New Generation", which I had planted. I had come to realize that young people wanted an environment where they are loved and accepted for who they were without the judgmental attitude of the church.

The idea that youth are a problem to society and to themselves is a central theme to which the media and researchers return. It is true that young people are generally seen as problematic and need to be **reined** in to keep them out of trouble, but it may be more about vision and passion and finding their path in life.

The young people are seldom seen as people who make a significant contribution to a nation though. They are often referred to as leaders of *tomorrow*, and in a church setting they would be referred to as tomorrow's church. I would argue and say that young people are already leaders and they are already a church. In other words, they are assets in any community.

Working in Khayelitsha was tough because I worked with hardly any financial support. It was hard to support my work and my family. Nevertheless, I was convinced that reaching out to the young people of Khayelitsha was the right thing to do.

At that time, I would hear about mission trips by white churches to places such as Mozambique, Botswana, etc. and wonder why they were not investing in Khayelitsha? If they cared about people far away, why not close by on their doorstep? There were very few whites who understood their position of privilege and contributed to the work in Khayelitsha.

The load became a bit lighter when Lorenzo Davids, the then CEO of Cape Town City Mission heard about the work I was doing. Lorenzo was introduced to me by the Wilmot's who were part of my support group in Somerset West.

He incorporated the youth work in Khayelitsha into the broader City Mission work without trying to micromanage me or 'use' me. It was nice to not work alone any longer. I became part of a team that was passionate about people. Years later, Lorenzo as CEO of Community Chest, was instrumental in helping me to get a scholarship for postgraduate studies in Community Development. He was present at my graduation and after shaking my hand, he prophesied that I would get my PhD. I certainly do not want to be the reason why his prophecy is not fulfilled!

It was in Khayelitsha that I met Xola Skosana who was working for a Christian Organization called 'Youth Alive'. Our passion for youth brought us together. We spent hours talking about our work and read lots of books that related to Christian ministry. As Christians do, we spent time in prayer, at times seeking divine intervention.

I soon realized that Xola was smart, a deep thinker and very troubled by the injustices of apartheid. He was an eloquent speaker and a keen athlete. He had participated in a couple of Comrades Marathons, 89 km distance between Pietermaritzburg and Durban. He likes to think that he is good looking too. I can't really comment on that, but I think his wife Ndumi would probably concur.

Xola's background is different to mine. He was born in a Port Elizabeth Township and either experienced or witnessed the gross brutality of apartheid's security agents. He was raised by a single parent in the midst of township misery. He would not be alive today in the environment that he grew up in, had he not been recruited to safe Christian spaces that were created to keep young people away from politics.

Years later, he discovered to his disgust that the whites' "messiah" who would recruit and proselytize young people was in fact hired and funded by the apartheid regime. The project was never about black lives. It was about keeping the regime intact and the perpetuation of an unjust system through religious distraction

So Xola, having grown up in an urban setting, was robbed of rural life experiences. I think it is a huge advantage for people to experience both worlds. Xola and I related to white people differently. He would be confrontational and even aggressive when addressing an issue of injustice whereas I, on the other hand, would be calm and diplomatic. I later discovered that his approach was more effective because white people would pay attention. I felt that my soft approach was not bearing fruit. I would console myself by telling him that perhaps both approaches were essential.

Perhaps his role was to crush them down first so that I could pick them up to go on a journey of transformation. I, suspect, though, that he is not convinced that my soft approach yields any fruit. He reckons that white people do not care about black people at all. Being the eternal optimist that I am, I choose hope, perhaps naively so.

In his book 'Things we feel and dare not say – disband the white church', this is what he says about me:

Theo and I had been friends for over five years by then. We first met in December 1996 when I was busy planting a church in Khayelitsha. In January 2006, he left for the Eastern Cape and established himself in a place called Willowvale, the home of the late Xhosa king, Xolilizwe Sigcawu. Theo left on a brave mission to explore a concept he calls "Ubuntu Village"- How should an African church look like in a rural setting? He took along with him a wealth of experience in multiracial and cross-cultural church work. He has served many organizations such as Africa Enterprise, City Mission, Transformation Africa, to mention just a few. He has travelled far and wide in search of working models, including the annual mass prayer rally of Dr Silvoso in Argentina. The two of us shared a deep passion for the preaching of the gospel, you could call us modern day zealots.

Together we read books on church growth such as a Purpose Driven Church by Rick Warren, a similar book by Ted Haggard and also attended conferences. This was all in search of the best working leadership models. We followed religiously the writings of Bill Hybels of Willow Creek, John Maxwell and many such renowned leaders. We used to often pray together in a church in Somerset West.

Theo was loved and esteemed by white people in church circles. I don't know if it's still the case since he began to question the relevance of the white church and challenging what he calls "White prescriptions to black problems. He was "the other black", like Mandela, or some of the radio presenters on SAFM who are dear darlings of white callers. In the minds of many white Christians, Theo was not like "those black people". He found himself walking a lonely road as one of the few black leaders in white Christian circles. We used to kid around when we talked on the phone, I would ask him about his whereabouts and he would be at some place with some Christian white friend/s. Then I would caution him to be careful and not drink too much wine.

How did I get to be this popular person in white circles? Well, it all started one early Monday morning breakfast at the Alphen Hotel in Constantia.

The Alphen Boutique Hotel in Cape Town is an historic building in the Constantia Valley, one of the country's oldest and most picturesque suburbs. The Constantia Valley is renowned for having some of the best vineyards in the Cape, as well as some of the oldest. In the hotel's advert they emphasize that the location of the Constantia hotel ensures that it is a convenient base to explore further afield such as Stellenbosch or the centre of Cape Town.

This five-star Alphen offers a quiet, relaxing atmosphere that is suitable for both leisure and business travelers. The advert continues to state that, "The leafy estate on which this gorgeous boutique hotel offers a fine dining restaurant, a sophisticated alfresco bar, outdoor facilities and conference venues. It ends with, "These places are popular with locals as well as guests at the hotel."

This is where I was introduced to the white world of Cape Town when I chose to leave Bizweni Church in the Somerset

West. I still had fresh experiences of my time in the US and Canada where I was treated mostly as an honorary white. In other words, I was treated as though I was not like the 'other blacks'.

The spacious hall at the Alphen was full of white people from different parts of Cape Town. I cannot recall why I ended up there that morning and what the topic of discussion was. I do recall, however, that a Black person stood up – he was the only black face in the audience besides me, and spoke so passionately about how fed up black people were with white arrogance and ill treatment. He went on to say that "Most black people I know would not hesitate to shoot a white person if they had a chance". I was uncomfortable and almost embarrassed by what was being said. I did not know any black person that "would not hesitate to shoot a white person".

After he sat down there was a bit of pause. I then stood up and said something to the effect that not all black people were full of hatred towards white people. I also said that some white people were good people and were opposed to white supremacy. I said that it was easy to be 'one' in Jesus. By the time I sat down white people were all smiling. I sensed a great deal of relief.

Looking back, I realize how ignorant I was about black pain and how blinded I was by the parts of Christian religion that trivializes the pain that millions of black people across the globe are experiencing due to institutionalized racism. Unfortunately, I never got to know the name of the black guest who made the above pronouncements. After the events of that morning and having had time to reflect, I felt a bit uneasy about my message of hope. I felt that I helped neutralize a message that should have been a wake-up call to white people who live in church bubbles, oblivious to the devastation caused by structural racism and apartheid.

I am embarrassed to say that this is how white people in Cape Town started to gravitate towards me; simply because I was in denial of the pain inflicted on my compatriots and me by the evil system. I was made numb by a Christian message that does not link Jesus to issues of justice. Yes, I even saw white privilege as 'white blessings'.

I think I was in deep denial that racism is present in the church. I believed that it is only found *outside* the church and belongs to non-Christians. I was confronted by a question that pastor Wilson Siko, a well-known Khayelitsha pastor, once asked me that got me thinking. He had just come out of a meeting with white colleagues and was a bit upset. In his anger, he said that he did not think that any white person would go to heaven. I quickly corrected him stating that not all white people were the same. He then asked me to mention one white person that I thought would go to heaven. My mind quickly went into overdrive thinking about all the white people I knew. The computer in my mind gave the error 404 – web page cannot be found. I was bothered by the fact that I could not mention one white person that I could put my neck on the block for and say, "so and so could not be racist, therefore he/she qualifies to go to heaven".

As Xola mentioned I got to a point where I felt suffocated. The Christianity that I was part of in Cape Town got into me and my system could not take it anymore. I was attending so many meetings in both the townships and suburbs in the white world and in the black world. I was confronted on a daily basis by gross inequality. For instance, I would attend a meeting in a leafy suburb of Constantia where the evidence of affluence was visible everywhere you looked. From the vehicles parked outside to the magnificent houses that could be mistaken for palaces. The next day I would be running a bible study in an informal settlement in Khayelitsha where poverty and suffering is the order of the day. I once wondered aloud if black and white people would be going to the same heaven.

I met Michael Louis, a prominent Cape Town businessperson, when he showed up at one of these meetings, driving the latest Jaguar that turned heads. Everyone shook Michael's hand, congratulating him and when it was my turn Michael looked rather uncomfortable. He said, "Well, people may ask why I am driving a car like this when there are hungry people?" I said nothing because I did not ask that question. Then he answered his own question as he moved on to the next person. "You have to think of safety, you know." As for me, I was not thinking of safety. I was wondering if my car had enough fuel to get me home.

The richest person that I worked with in Cape Town was Graham Power, the CEO of Power Group Companies. Graham was the man behind what started as Cape Town Transformation, a prayer movement. Trevor Pearce, an Anglican Minister, formed the initial group together with other ministers, before Graham and others got involved. Power, with his massive resources and financial muscle, was able to grow the movement exponentially until it reached all corners of the globe. By then it was called 'The Global Day of Prayer'.

I was asked by Graham Power to help on a part-time basis. I earned more in my part-time job than I did in the full-time job, with lots of benefits too, including a company car, garage card, a cell phone and even a 13th cheque. I think I was the envy of many township pastors. I also did a lot of travelling across the globe. Part of my job was to mobilize people for the Day of Prayer.

I think the first major mistake was to have a prayer gathering on Human Rights Day, which is 21st March. The gathering had more people than those that attended gatherings organized by government – approximately 50 000. Needless to say, the ANC was furious and felt that this prayer movement was undermining the efforts of government to honor this day.

Even though this gathering was multiracial, there was an overwhelming number of white attendees, who would not normally attend gatherings on Human Rights Day.

The late Minister Kader Asmal took the organizers to task with all the media frenzy that went with it. Some Christian believers also believed that it was insensitive of the movement to have a prayer rally on the 21st of March. Lorenzo Davids, the then CEO of the City Mission had this to say about the event, "This is an arrogant display of white power."

The prayer day was shifted to a different date. This presented me with my first exposure to large gatherings. I was always on the program and would appear on TV doing interviews. I developed celebrity status and wherever I went people would tell me that I looked familiar!

A man called Dawie Spangenberg and I crisscrossed the country visiting towns and cities mobilizing churches for the Day of Prayer. Dawie was a businessperson who was giving part of his time to the movement. Sometimes I would travel alone for many hours to far-flung areas of our country to spread awareness. I had a sense that Graham, who was a relatively new Christian then, had an expectation that the day of prayer would simply solve all South Africa's problems. He once shared how he believes that even HIV AIDS could be overcome through these prayers.

. . .

His favourite verse was Isaiah 66:8 which reads as follows:

Who has heard of such things? Who has ever seen things like this? Can a country be born in a day or a nation be brought forth in a moment?

Graham would read this verse whenever he had an opportunity to address people. Graham and I flew to England and then Sweden together to raise funds for the movement.

We hardly spoke on the plane. I would from time-to-time ask him a question and would receive short answers. It really felt uncomfortable to travel with someone with whom you could not have a conversation.

When we arrived at Heathrow airport, we met up with Dawie Spangenberg, a long-time friend of his. Dawie had taken an earlier flight from OR Tambo airport as he was from Gauteng.

He had been a soldier in the South African Defense Force under the apartheid rule. He then started his own security company, which did so well that Dawie ended up being labelled a 'Businessperson of the Year', which was how he ended up meeting Graham Power.

Graham had received the same award in the previous year. I found it easy to have a conversation with Dawie and we would cover all manner of subjects. It was through this that I got to know the extent of Graham's extreme wealth. Dawie would try to convince me that the Afrikaners are not as bad as they are made out to be. He thought the English-speaking people were the bad ones.

He pointed this out again when a police officer stopped me at the airport apparently to search my baggage but when he realized I was travelling with white people he let me go. Dawie did not seem to believe that there is such a thing as white privilege; he would argue he had worked hard for what he had. It was impossible to have a conversation with him about structural racism, let alone black pain. Dawie was fun to be with but he still had a long way to go, and I had no appetite to take him there.

As soon as we met Dawie at Heathrow, Graham became alive and he and Dawie talked quite loudly in a mixture of English and Afrikaans while I watched enviously, conscious of my inferior status in this team. I was left to look after the baggage when they wandered off to buy coffee. While they were gone, a stranger approached me and pretended to be asking for something. Before I answered, he was gone.

It turned out that this chap was a decoy because when my companions arrived Dawie immediately noticed that his laptop was gone with six hundred pounds inside the bag! We had been mugged. It turned out that England was not what we thought it was. Dawie, a heavyset guy, was fuming. He looked around helplessly, ready to do some bodily damage to the culprit while Graham calmed him down.

We then rushed out of the terminus building to catch a taxi that would take us to the SA *Gemeente* Church, which is run and attended by white Afrikaans-speaking South Africans who live in London.

Attending an Afrikaans-speaking church in the middle of London was quite intriguing. I apparently fell asleep in the middle of the sermon and snored, according to Dawie!

Graham and I would return separately from overseas.

Graham Power was known to be a generous giver. I know he poured many of his own resources into the prayer movement. Nevertheless, he never really endorsed the notion of restitution. I guess he preferred helping others while being the person who benefited immensely because of an unjust system that favored his race.

His actions could have been an act of repentance that compensates for the acts of injustices of colonialism and apartheid. If that is the case, the giver becomes humble as opposed to being arrogant expecting to be elevated.

Graham Power was quite fond of me when I was part of the Transformations' Movement and wanted me to be present at most of the movement's events. He personally wanted me to be the narrator of the promotional video of the Transformation's Movement. There was once an attempt to replace me with a person that the media people thought had a better voice than mine and that was unsuccessful.

I must admit that there were some awkward times when I worked with the movement. One of those times was when we had meetings with people from across the country. I would notice that white people, particularly the Afrikaners, had a tendency of greeting women with a kiss on the lips. I would observe people around me greeting and kissing, and I would often be the only black person in the group, thus the odd one out. I would wonder whether I should do what other men are doing or just shake hands.

I think a couple of times I tried to imitate others and greeted with a kiss. I always felt uncomfortable doing this and had a sense that the women I greeted in this manner felt the same. Eventually I came up with a plan. I would keep away when people meet and greet each other and only slip back in quietly when everyone had settled down. I had gathered that shaking a white man's hand was probably enough and already a huge achievement!

There were some lighter moments too during the Transformation days. I recall visiting the town of Hopefield.

Hopefield is a settlement in the West Coast District Municipality in the Western Cape province of South Africa on the R45 between Malmesbury and Vredenburg. The town is east of Saldanha Bay and Langebaan, 40 km southeast of Vredenburg and 120 km north of Cape Town.

The town has a population of about 6000 people, and more than 80 percent would be classified as coloured in South Africa. I got so much attention in this town at the Christian gathering we had! The people here simply loved everything about me and I was told that so much of me resembles Jesus! This is something I would remind my family about over and over! Moreover, the sound of my voice was described as soothing. It was not the first time I had been told this. A white woman once told me this after a big gathering where I was one of the speakers. She went on to say, "I can listen to your voice over and over."

It turned out that it is not only my voice that is soothing. My wife Thandi tells me that my snoring soothes her too. I know of someone who would vehemently disagree with her and that is Wilhelm Verwoerd, the grandson of Hendrik Verwoerd. Wilhelm and I once shared a room when we were attending a Restitution Workshop at Mike Winfield's home on the west coast. I had warned him before we went to bed that I was a snorer. Wilhelm did not seem to mind or perhaps he did not know how to respond.

When I woke up in the middle of the night, I instinctively looked in the direction of his bed to see if he was ok. The bed was empty. I hoped that perhaps he had gone to the toilet and would be coming back but he never did! I felt guilty for having caused him such inconvenience having to wake up and seek a bed elsewhere, but then I comforted myself by thinking this was nothing compared to what his people did to us, particularly his grandfather who is the architect of apartheid. I then closed my eyes and went back to sleep peacefully. Wilhelm had gone down to sleep in the lounge his explanation was that he wanted to be close to the toilet!

In 2005 I had started to feel that I had had enough of Cape Town and all the work that was associated with it. I felt really exhausted and needed a break, a long break. I kept thinking of the words that my friend Andiswa Flatela, a medical doctor, once said.

She had reminded me that white people see us as projects. I was realizing that my relationships with the white "friends" were very superficial and that I was more like a project. I longed for village life and longed to live a life of Ubuntu. I wanted deep connections with people. I felt that something was missing.

After agonizing over this for a long time, I convinced my family that it was time to leave Cape Town and head to the Eastern Cape. I was not even sure what I would be doing there.

I will not bore the reader with all the little details, but I ended up leading a Bible school and a church in Willowvale, close to the wild coast. That was not the initial plan. I had made the mistake of believing politicians when they sounded like they were genuinely concerned about the plight of the poor. I got a rude awakening.

My dream of an UBUNTU VILLAGE never materialized. In addition, I spent eight years trying to change a religion-focused institution into a community-focused entity, with no success.

I was becoming disillusioned with religion as my family life was also disintegrating. I finally lost my job and got divorced from Jesika. I headed to my home village in Ngcobo with nothing left. I went back to my mother's arms who was then close to 75 years old. It felt so good to still have a home and a mother. My older sister who is also named Thandi looked after her.

I tried to connect with the village folks but my being umfundisi (pastor or teacher?) was a huge barrier. I was labelled a "holy man'. Nevertheless, I continued to do Ubuntu acts providing skills to others. I am thankful to those who continued believing in me and supporting my work.

In 2016, I got an invitation from JL Zwane Presbyterian Church in Gugulethu to serve as an associate minister with Reverend Dr. Spiwo Xapile. My new wife Thandi joined me as we began a new chapter as a couple and community development practitioners under the guidance of umfundisi Xapile. This church exposed us to the NGO world and the wonderful work that NGOs are doing. I did still believe that the church has a critical role to play in community development, especially the white Church in the spirit of Restitution.

When Graham Power heard that I was back in Cape Town in 2016, he requested a meeting with me. We met at his headquarters in Blackheath. He seemed quite delighted to see me after a long time and expressed surprise that my hair had not turned grey, perhaps forgetting that I was almost a decade younger than him and others on his team!

His office had not changed much since the days I used to frequent it. It was as plush as ever, I noticed additional photos on the walls, and my attention was drawn to the one where Graham seemed to be meeting the pope.

There was also a certificate of an honorary doctorate that he was awarded, I think by a foreign university. I remembered that I used to feature in some of the photos in his office. I was not sure if that was still the case, as I did not want to make it obvious that I was checking things out.

He asked me how I was doing and about my family. I shared with him that I was doing well, that I had been through some challenging times including a divorce, and that I was beginning a new life. He did not seem surprised and I could not detect any emotions.

The conversation must have lasted less than ten minutes and then he held both my hands, - I could not help noticing how hairy his arms were - and prayed for me. I cannot remember what the prayer was about, but it felt superficial. The whole meeting was rather cold and a bit uncomfortable. Graham gave me two books, one about him and the Transformation Movement and the other by some American prosperity gospel protagonist. He expressed hope that I would enjoy reading those books and that I would be blessed. We then shook hands and I was released.

Gone were the days when I used to leave his office with big promises and sometimes with a big cheque! I felt that the meeting was simply meant to show that I was no longer needed and that hurt! I shared this with Umfundisi Xapile, my mentor, who simply smiled and allowed me to wrestle with it. I read the book about the story of Transformation Movement hoping that I would see my name feature somewhere given the role I thought I had played. It did not appear anywhere.

The dream of an UBUNTU VILLAGE has not disappeared. I am dreaming of an initiation school at my home village in Gotyubeni for white people who may want to journey towards being truly African. It is my intention that these conversations will start in a black township of Khayelitsha, Cape Town, and spread to a rural set up of the former Transkei.

I am inviting white people who may be interested in such dialogues.

PART TWO

"Being White: De Gruchy and Verwoerd."

CHAPTER SEVEN

I t was a beautiful Saturday morning when I jumped into my car to honor a 10h00 appointment in Voelmoed near Hermanus. I felt honoured that this retired professor had agreed to meet with me. I had never met him prior to this appointment.

I wanted to interview him because of a lecture he had given at Rondebosch United Church about white South African males. The title of his lecture was the following:

IS IT POSSIBLE FOR A WHITE SOUTH AFRICAN MALE TO ENTER THE KINGDOM OF HEAVEN?

I was delighted when my friend Dr Robert Steiner provided me with his contact details so I could ask for an appointment. I enjoyed the drive on the N2 from Cape Town towards Hermanus, passing the towns of Somerset West and the Strand where I used to reside years back. I am always amazed to see how these towns have grown so exponentially over the last several years. Lwandle hostel where I started my community work no longer exists, instead it is a sprawling township that boasts a number of schools and health facilities. A far cry from what it was when I started working there and helped to start the first school. I always think of Mr Rasmeni when I drive past this area and often wonder about what happened to him.As I climbed the steep Sir Lowry's Pass, my C4 turbo kicked in enabling me to climb the mountain effortlessly in top gear. On the other side of the mountain, I drove past Siyanyanzela informal settlement on the left. You can hardly see the settlement from the road. It has a growing population of a couple of thousands who came to the town of Grabouw to look for better pastures. The majority of those living there come from the homelands such as the Transkei and Ciskei. The homeland system was not sustainable.I drove past the famous Peregrine Convenience store to the right and past a little road that I used to take when invited to preach at the small Elgin United Church when they could not afford to call a minister. As I headed towards Houw Hoek the road sign "The Valley" on the right is another little road that I used to take to visit George and Lettie Strachan on their farm who were firm supporters of the work I was doing. After effortlessly climbing to the top of the Houw Hoek Mountains, Bot River appears at the bottom on the right. This is how the town is described online.

The small, picturesque village of Botriver lies in the foothills of the Houw Hoek Mountains, en route to Hermanus. The Bot River, after which the hamlet is named, meanders its way through a fertile valley surrounded by mountains covered in fynbos, historical wine farms and fields of wheat.

A place of crossing in the Bot River originally served as a spot for bartering butter with the Khoi-khoi tribes and the river was attributed with the name 'butter' from both sides - the Afrikaans word for butter is 'botter' and the Khoi-khoi called it 'Couga', which means 'lots of butter'. The name stuck and today this river flows through the town into a large lagoon, which forms a marsh at its mouth. These wetlands are home to thousands of waterfowl and one of the only remaining herds of wild horses is said to roam the area. Botriver has a tradition of accommodating travellers. The Bot River Hotel was built in the 1890s and today serves as a drop-off point for the Baz Bus shuttle - a hop-on and hop-off backpacker shuttle that offers travellers of all ages a way to explore South Africa.

A whole generation of South Africans were introduced to the town of Botriver as the setting for a popular TV series - 'Nommer Asseblief' (number please), and visitors used to insist on seeing the telephone exchange and meeting the characters from the soapie.

Bot River also has an informal settlement called New France that has many challenges similar to those faced by other South African Towns and cities, such as inadequate services and unemployment. I had the privilege of working with the New France community as part of my work with Violence Prevention through Urban Upgrading (VPUU).

VPUU is a great organization that aims to overcome the different levels of economic, cultural, social, institutional and spatial exclusion, in order to reduce and prevent crime.

Based on a structured, participatory approach, the focus is on improving safety, providing public services, and developing social cohesion factors, community data and the willingness of the local community and other partners to cooperate in implementing a transformation programme, through facilitating processes between communities, government departments and other organisations.

In Bot River I took the R43 towards Hermanus, a thriving holiday resort offering residents and holiday makers all modern amenities yet retaining its angler's village charm. The popular resort town of Hermanus, situated between mountain and sea, has gained worldwide recognition as the world's foremost land-based whale-watching destination. This has resulted in the former fishing village showing tremendous growth over the last few years.

Contributory factors to the success of the town are the natural scenic beauty, the mild climate, the range of outdoor activities available, and the close proximity to accommodation in Cape Town, with Hermanus being a mere 140 km from the Cape Metropole. The ideal base from which to explore the Western Cape and the Cape Overberg.

Hermanus has something for everyone. The Fernkloof Nature Reserve has over 40 km of walks, ranging from moderate to strenuous walks in the beautiful mountains, which form an imposing backdrop to the town. The 14 km of unique cliff walks recently incorporated into the nature reserve boast a variety of coastal fynbos and birdlife.

The pristine stretches of beach offer solitude to the walker and boating activities abound in the Klein River Lagoon, renowned for its birdlife. Invigorating horse rides along the beach appeal to all ages. The Hermanus Golf Course is well known and curious baboons create a diversion as they silently observe the players.

The Old Harbour complex in Hermanus offers the visitor an insight into Hermanus past as a Fisherman's village and marine life.

Hermanus and neighbouring towns Onrus and Stanford are the residence of a variety of artists, from watercolours, to writers, potters and crafters. The Hermanus Wine Route, the southernmost in Africa, produces top quality, world renowned wines. Hermanus is firmly established on the Epicurean map with its myriad of restaurants, fine wine, fresh vegetables cheese and fish. Today Hermanus remains a thriving holiday resort, offering residents and holiday makers all modern amenities yet retaining its angler's village charm.

VOLMOED

It is close to this quaint but bustling town that we find Volmoed. Set in its own little valley of 130 hectares of fynbos, Volmoed offers a peaceful venue for individuals, family holidays, weddings, conferences and church retreats, as well as accommodation. As the Onrust River makes its way from the heights of Babylon's Toring through De Bos Dam it tumbles down into this little valley with a waterfall and lovely natural rock pool, setting the scene of tranquility and natural beauty that are the hallmarks of this Retreat and Conference Centre.

I arrived here about 30 minutes early. I was a bit familiar with the place because I had been here twice before. My first visit was with the VPUU (Violence Prevention through Urban Upgrading) team lead by its CEO Michael Krause. Our team had spent a few days navigating the difficult terrain of transformation in the workplace. The VPUU team was wrestling with this important topic with the assistance of a Cape Town-based service provider.

My second visit was a very brief one. I was en route to Caledon with my family, having stopped at The Grail in Kleinmond to greet my colleague Priscilla Erasmus. I wanted to introduce my wife Thandi to some of my colleagues and show her some of the places where I visit and work. My former colleague and friend at JL Zwane in Gugulethu Rev Spiwo Xapile would always tell me about the importance of exposing our spouses to the work that we do.

After parking my car, I was directed to John's house. "The last house at the top of the hill… I hope you are fit enough." I was warned. I was quite sure it would be a breeze because I try to walk six kilometres every morning. But it was a tough climb to the top. When I arrived at the house, a tall bearded man who looked to be in his seventies met me. He looked friendly and welcoming. His wife stood next to him; he introduced her as Isobel. The bespectacled chap led me to his lounge full of shelves stacked with books. It was not hard to tell that this was the dwelling of a professor.

For many years, De Gruchy was a Robert Selby Taylor Professor of Christian Studies at University of Cape Town. He remains an Emeritus Professor at the University of Cape Town and holds a post as an Extraordinary Professor at the University of Stellenbosch. A festschrift was published in his honour in 2002. Some of his earliest works were written in the midst of apartheid in South Africa, speaking out against the legislation and engaging the theology of Dietrich Bonhoeffer to argue for the liberation of the oppressed. After apartheid legislation was abolished in 1991, de Gruchy wrote a number of works speaking about the theological role of art in society and advocating for a theology of reconciliation.

This was my first encounter with the retired professor, and he wanted to know many things about me. While we were chatting, Isobel reappeared and offered us tea. I was not here to tell Professor De Gruchy about myself. I wanted to interview him regarding the memorial lecture that he had given at the

Rondebosch United Church in honour of his son Stephen De Gruchy. As mentioned earlier the tittle of the lecture was

IS IT POSSIBLE FOR A WHITE SOUTH AFRICAN MALE TO ENTER THE KINGDOM OF HEAVEN.

I am afraid the interview did not go so well. De Gruchy was so keen to know about what my Xhosa name means and more about me! He then went on to talk about his involvement with Hermanus Varsity, which I had heard of. As a Community Development Practitioner, I was also very keen to hear about a bold initiative that was taken by the residents of Hermanus to offer tertiary education to the less privileged inhabitants of this town. I was encouraged by the pivotal role that he played in establishing this admirable project. I wrapped up the "interview" by asking his permission to include his lecture in my book. He agreed on condition that I would promise to be involved with the Varsity when I moved to Botriver. I had shared with him that I would like to live in Botriver one day.

As we were about to shake hands to say our goodbyes, we remembered that we cannot do that because of Covid-19. He gave me a copy of one of his latest books with the tittle "I HAVE COME A LONG WAY." I devoured all 280 pages of it in two days.

It would be unfair to take you straight to the lecture without being introduced to John's late son Steve De Gruchy. His premature death was a tremendous loss to South Africa and indeed the world over. This prompted Archbishop Desmond Tutu to entitle one of Steve's memorial lectures that he gave, as

"God is God's worst enemy."

Steve de Gruchy was a keynote speaker at the Towards Effective Anglican Mission conference in March 2007 in

Boksburg, South Africa, and the Episcopal Church's Everyone, Everywhere world mission conference in June 2008 in Baltimore, Maryland.

O'Neill, who helped to organize the TEAM conference, said de Gruchy had the ability "to strike to the core of an issue and render action both obvious and imperative. I am just one of countless thousands whom he reached as a teacher -- he has been an inspiration to me. His words and writings are a precious legacy to carry into the future."

The author of more than 20 books and research papers, de Gruchy's three main areas of writing were social history of Christianity in South Africa; theology and development; and religion and public health.

Mary Brennan, the Episcopal Church's mission communication officer and an organizer of the Everyone, Everywhere conference, described de Gruchy as "a remarkable man and a joy to be around. His insight on the connectedness of people and their actions in carrying out God's mission in the world never failed to energize anyone who had the opportunity to hear him speak. The global mission community has lost a thoughtful, dynamic leader."

From 1987-94, de Gruchy served as a chaplain at Groote Schuur Hospital and was minister of Gleemoor Congregational Church in Athlone, Cape Town, before becoming director of the Moffat Mission Trust in Kuruman, a position he held until 2000. He was appointed the first full-time director of the theology and development program at the University of KwaZulu-Natal in July 2000.

According to biographical information on the University of KwaZulu-Natal website, de Gruchy "always had a lively academic and practical interest in the interface between the

Christian faith and social ethics." The website noted that during his student years at the University of Cape Town he served on the Student Representative Council, was active in the student anti-apartheid movement, a signatory to the Kairos Document, and a conscientious objector to military service.

"His work in the under-resourced rural area of Kuruman continued this focus where he helped establish NGOs working in the field of land rights, small business development, early childhood development, and leadership training," the website says. Most recently, de Gruchy had been engaged in research work on the interface between religion and health in Africa in the context of the HIV/AIDS pandemic.In addition to his participation at the TEAM and Everyone, Everywhere conferences, de Gruchy had spoken at many church-related events on issues concerning theology, mission, development and poverty.Ecumenically, de Gruchy had been involved with the World Council of Churches' Justice, Peace and Creation team, the World Alliance of Reformed Churches, the Council for World Mission, the International Congregational Fellowship and the Church Unity Commission in South Africa. Below is Steve's

STEVE'S OBITUARY:

South African theologian, author and activist Steve de Gruchy drowned Feb. 21 while river tubing with his son in the Natal Midlands near the Drakensburg Mountains. He was 48. Police divers and dogs on Feb. 24 reportedly recovered de Gruchy's body 700 meters downstream from where he had last been seen alive. "Steve contributed so much. From the church's role in the struggle against apartheid to helping define a theology for social activism and transformation," said Janette O'Neill, senior director of Africa programs for Episcopal Relief & Development. "Above all, he was a talented and generous teacher. "Born in Durban on Nov. 16, 1961, de Gruchy went on to become an ordained minister in the United Congregational Church of Southern Africa and professor of theology and development at the University of KwaZulu-Natal in Pietermaritzburg. He also served as head of the School of Religion and Theology at the university and editor of the Journal of Theology for Southern Africa since 2003.

Now I want to take the reader to a packed hall at the Rondebosch United Church in Cape Town to listen to Steve's father deliver a lecture at his son's memorial.

CHAPTER EIGHT

The 8th Steve de Gruchy Memorial Lecture,

Cape Town - 30 April 2019

INTRODUCTION

Judging from comments I received since the topic of my lecture was announced, it seems to have touched a sensitive nerve. Some people said they would only attend if I answered the question in the affirmative, and others said the answer had to be "no"! One person wrote, "if you think that is a difficult question, how about 'can a white male homophobic Dutch Reformed Afrikaner *dominee* enter the kingdom of God?'" Yet another said it was a stupid question. Yet judging from the number of white, male South Africans present here this evening, it seems as if there is great interest in finding out about how they can be saved from the wrath to come. And, I confess, I also have some personal interest in the subject.

The question is, certainly a personal one and obviously theological as well. But it is also of social and political importance in thinking about the future place and role of white males in South Africa not least as we face a general election next week. But why single out white males as though we are a distinct tribe and have a favored place in society and unique role to fulfil? Why give us a special status and further inflate our egos? Or, some might say, why pick on us, exposing our faults and failures, accusing us of being part of the problem, and make us feel more guilty? We are not the only ones to blame for what is wrong! Just leave us alone and led us mingle with everyone else, and hopefully lose our white maleness in the crowd!

Of course, we should not generalize, for not all white South African males are the same. Some are English-speaking, others Afrikaans; some are poorer than others, some very rich; some are Christian, others Jewish and yet others secular; some come from good schools others not; some are gay, others not; some come from loving and caring families, others from dysfunctional families. And, as is true of all people whether white males or not, some are born with more gifts and talents than others, some have had greater opportunities, some are shy, and others outgoing. And some have inherited long-life genes, others not. All types and conditions apply to white male South Africans, as they do to other groups.

But, of course, if you are white, male and *gay* you are certainly not part of the white male macho network. In years past you had to stay within the closet whether at school or college, whether in business and the workplace, whether on the sports-field or in the club house, in the army and the church. Gay white male South Africans may have been privileged as white males under apartheid, but if they did not play by the homophobic rules of the time they were ridiculed and excluded. In fact, playing by the rules, being part of the old boys' network, made it exceedingly difficult for those who were non-conformists, whether gay or not. Yes, there are many variables within our tribe, except for the fact that we are all white, male and living in South Africa.

So, let me say four things at the outset about my topic.

1. While my focus is on white, male South Africans, my question is also inclusive, for how can anyone, irrespective of race, gender and nationality enter the kingdom of heaven? If you are not a white male, you can and should still ask the question for yourself and I hope you do.
2. My question is specifically about white males because they were largely responsible for creating and sustaining colonialism and apartheid, and we have done so because we have had a privileged place in society and were empowered to do so.
3. It is also specifically about white males because many regard them as a liability if not an embarrassment in public, business and academic life, rather than an asset.
4. As a reminder that there have been and still are remarkable white male South Africans who have risen above their race, gender and class, and played – as they continue to do – an important role in working for a more just South Africa.

I could add a fifth preliminary comment, of course, because this lecture is in honour of the memory of Steve de Gruchy and he was a white male South African. So, I think the topic is appropriate and that he would approve of my choice. Undoubtedly, he would also think that he could deliver a better lecture on the subject, but sadly he can't any longer. But did Steve enter the kingdom of heaven? If he did, then it must be possible for any white South African male to do so and we could all have a glass of wine and go home. But there might be an uproar of disapproval in this assembly. Some shouting "no, he didn't!" others, "how can we know for sure?" and yet others, "what does it mean to enter the kingdom of heaven anyway?" I might even be accused of avoiding that question and getting you here under false pretensions on a cold night. So, I must continue.

But this is a difficult lecture to give. How I wish Steve was still alive to do so instead. We do miss him so much! But I must put emotion aside and accept the task with gratitude. For how many fathers are asked to give a lecture in honoured remembrance of their son? How many fathers have had a son who was such an exceptional and talented man, and whose memory has been celebrated in this way for the past eight years by distinguished lecturers? So, despite the emotional challenge I accept the task gratefully because I think Steve would want me to, and I think he would have approved of the topic and if he delivered it he would have done so with that characteristic impish grin on his face that always told his parents that he was up to some mischief. And as he was also a preacher, I begin with a passage from Scripture.

AN IMPOSSIBLE POSSIBILITY

Jesus looked around and said to his disciples, "How hard it will be for those who have wealth to enter the kingdom of God!" And the disciples were perplexed at these words. But Jesus said to them again, "How hard it is to enter the kingdom of God! It is easier for a camel to go through the eye of a needle than for someone who is rich to enter the kingdom of God. They were greatly astounded and said to one another, "Then who can be saved?" Jesus looked at them and said, "with mortals it is impossible, but not for God; for God, all things are possible."

— MARK 10:23-27

This interaction between Jesus and his disciples occurred after a rich young man came to Jesus and asked him "Good teacher, what must I do to inherit eternal life?" Jesus told him to keep the commandments. The man replied that he had done so since his youth. Jesus looked at him and, as the gospel tells us, "loved him." But there was one thing he still had to do. He had to sell all his possessions and give his money to the poor. Downcast, he turned away. That was a bridge too far. The cost of entering the kingdom of heaven was too great.

This story played a decisive role in the conversion of St. Francis of Assisi, for he, too, was the privileged son of a rich businessman. But there came the day when he did what the young man in Jesus' story did not do, he gave up his inheritance and followed Jesus like a poor beggar. We may admire St. Francis, but few of us follow his example in renouncing privilege to follow Christ and enter the kingdom of heaven. A comparable story is told of Henri Nouwen, the well-known writer of books on spirituality, who left his comfortable position as a university chaplain in Boston to live in solidarity among the poor in Latin America. But once there, he discovered that it was impossible to identify with them fully. Unlike them, he always knew he could escape the daily grind of poverty, and that he always had a way out. Eventually he did so, returning to live in Boston.

We don't think less of Nouwen for opting out. At least he tried, which is more than most of us manage to do. In fact, most of us who are privileged have diluted Jesus' teaching to such an extent that Christianity has become "cheap grace" as Dietrich Bonhoeffer called it. The Christian life has been reduced to being happy, fulfilled, and achieving success. I do not decry these values for to be happy, fulfilled and successful is to be blessed, but they are not specifically Christian. The truth is, Jesus' teaching goes against the grain of privileged life, whether ancient, or modern. Even if we resist turning Christianity into a "prosperity cult." we still find it very difficult, if not impossible, to follow Jesus' path of costly discipleship. His teaching on forgiveness, reconciliation, love for one's enemies and solidarity in the struggles and suffering of the poor, is difficult, if not, as some say, impractical in the "real world".

Steve wrote his doctoral dissertation on the work of the American theologian Reinhold Niebuhr. And from Niebuhr he learnt that the teaching of Jesus is an impossible possibility. No one can follow Jesus' teaching fully, Niebuhr says, it is an impossibility because the "ethical demands made by Jesus are incapable of fulfilment" in our world.[1] And yet, by the grace of God, said Niebuhr, the impossible can become possible, and sometimes does. The teaching of Jesus may be an "impossible possibility", but he would not have invited us to enter the kingdom of heaven if it were not possible to do so. But how many of us who call ourselves Christians actually try to follow Jesus? How many of us are therefore serious about entering the kingdom of heaven whether we are white, male South Africans or not?

THE KINGDOM OF HEAVEN

My question is not only gender and racially specific, or socially and politically significant, it is also theological because it has to do with "entering the kingdom of heaven" – it is not about whether white South African males can obtain a visa to visit the United States or the United Kingdom; it is not about whether they can become Australians and live in Perth, or emigrate to Canada; it is not about whether they can attend the University of Cape Town or Limpopo; it is not about who they can marry, whether they can own property, or should receive the same salary as anybody else. It is not about whether they are better than others at sport or academics. It is specifically about whether they can "enter the kingdom of heaven." What, then, is the "kingdom of heaven?"

The "kingdom of heaven" as understood in the Bible does not refer to a place called "heaven" to which some, if not all of us, go when we die, whether white or black, male or female. In the Bible the word "heaven" is a synonym for God. Orthodox Jews were forbidden from uttering the word "God" because that would be taking God's name in vain and breaking the first commandment. So, instead of referring to the kingdom of God, they spoke about the "kingdom of heaven." If you read the gospels, that when Jesus talks about the kingdom of God or heaven, he is talking about how we are to live here and now. When he says his kingdom is not of this world, he is not saying that it has nothing to do with the world. He is saying that it is not subject to the authority of this world, just as he is not.

Let me introduce a helpful insight here which I have learnt from Bonhoeffer. It is the distinction he makes between the "ultimate" and the "penultimate." The ultimate is being justified by God, or "being saved" as some would say, with life after death in mind. This is beyond the control of any of us because it is a matter of God's grace. According to the gospel, nobody, whether white or black, male or female, South African, German, Brit, Brazilian or Burundian can be saved by their good works. The good news of Jesus Christ is that salvation is a gift of amazing grace. That is the ultimate which God alone makes possible. But we do have a say when it comes to the penultimate, that is, the "things before the last things," by doing what God asks of us here and now. So, if eternal salvation is your concern this evening as a white male, rest assured that is in the hands of God. And fortunately, God's grace is sufficient even when it comes to us.

God's amazing grace, then, is the ultimate. The penultimate, by contrast, is about life lived here and now. It is about the way in which we fulfil our responsibility in this world, it is about entering the kingdom of God today in this life not just the next. It is about doing the will of God today, living life responsibly before God. That is clear from the story of the rich man who came to Jesus. He wanted to know how he could live his life in accordance with God's will. Jesus tells him to keep the commandments. That he has done, the man replies. Well and good, says Jesus, you might have kept them literally by not stealing, committing adultery, or coveting your neighbour's ass or BMW Series 6, but you have failed to keep the intention of God's commandments. They are not just about what you should "not" do, they are more importantly, about what you "must" do. Love your neighbour as yourself, love even your enemy, seek God's justice before all else, go the extra mile, forgive seventy-times seventy, and take up your cross.

So, my question: "Can a white South African male enter the kingdom of heaven – or God?" is not about whether we white South African males can be saved and go to heaven when we die, but whether we can do God's will while we live. Are we able to "seek first God's kingdom and his justice before everything else?" Can us prodigal sons get out of the pigsty of male privilege and find a way to join the family back home? Can we, who have squandered our inheritance become brothers with the rest of humanity rather than think we are a favoured tribe entitled to inherit the earth? Can a white South African male be liberated from clinging to privilege and power to participate with everyone else in making South Africa a country that reflects God's kingdom of justice, reconciliation and peace? Or should we throw in the towel, go on a white male binge, or try to save our souls by emigrating to the kingdom of heaven in Trump-land, Brexit Britain, or Wonderland Dubai?

So, my question is this: are white South African males too much trapped in their privileged past, too much part of the problem to be of any use going forward? Will history eventually cast us aside as relics with no role in the present and no place in the future? Would it not be prudent to wash our hands of the problem and walk away, as did the rich young ruler? Do we have a meaningful role to play with everyone else in making this country more just, compassionate, peaceful and beautiful? It may seem an impossibility, but is it perhaps possible? Can a leopard change its spots, probably not? But a fat-cat juicy caterpillar can become a beautiful butterfly unless squashed underfoot. Such a transformation is possible, but it requires rebirth, and a necessary prelude to rebirth is the need to acknowledge our privileged status, for without doing so we will not see the need to change and have the courage and will to do so.

ACKNOWLEDGING PRIVILEGE, RACISM AND PATRIARCHY

Being a white South African male meant that Steve, like most of the rest of us in this category, was privileged. The only downside of being a white male under apartheid was that you were liable to be conscripted into the army. As a result, many paid the ultimate price with their lives, many others were physically disabled, and many, many others were psychologically damaged brutalized by their experiences on the border and in the townships. The psychological and social consequences of that senseless war are still very much part of the problem we face today, not least among those white males who were part of the military machine and the security apparatus. I know this from personal experience in counselling some of them.

Nonetheless, being white and male was a privileged status. We could get a good school and tertiary education, use good sporting facilities and, when we turned eighteen, we had the vote and could more easily rise to positions of power and influence in the public arena. And not least, job reservation meant that we could easily find employment. Yes, apartheid was all about white male economic empowerment. That might no longer be the case, but we, the previously advantaged, haven't done too badly since 1994. In fact, in many ways we are still privileged in a world where racism often reigns and violence against women is rampant.

Being white, black or brown is obviously a matter of skin colour. Apartheid was built on skin colour, on how a person looked, not on intelligence, education, profession, wealth, sporting ability, artistic or musical talent – it was all a matter of skin colour. Being white, black or brown is what mattered, and determined your fate. Apartheid made it impossible to be colour-blind, and even today that is still very difficult to achieve. Racism is deeply ingrained. But while race is real it is not scientific. The notion of "race" – as distinct from ethnicity or culture – was an ancient European invention associated with "darkest Africa," the mysterious "other."

Scientifically the pigment of our skins has to do with whether our ancestors had too much or too little sun. It is a matter if evolutionary adaptation. As Desmond Tutu once said, white people are rather "colourless". Our ancestors had too little sunshine, which may also be why we cannot all sing and dance as well as our compatriots who have benefitted from a surfeit of Vitamin D. But while race may not be scientific, it is a social and political reality that has serious consequences. It may be a myth created by Europeans over the centuries to justify conquest, slavery and colonialism, but saying so does not get rid of the effects of colonial conquest and slavery. The great Swiss theologian Karl Barth put it well:

"When members of the white race all enjoy every possible intellectual and material advantage on the basis of the superiority of one race and the subjection of many other races, and of the use that for centuries our race has made of both… My share in the sin against Africa or Asia for the last hundred or fifty years may be very remote or indirect, but would Europe be what it is, and would I be what I am, if that expansion had never happened…I did not take it from anybody, but simply inherited it by law…….[2]

Yes, racism is a powerful myth concocted to justify the way things are, just like the caste-system in India, or the class-system in the United Kingdom. It has little to do with ability, but everything to do with birth, inheritance, the way you look and the way you speak. There are those who are born to be servants, and those who are born to rule. This was the ugly lie that fed colonialism and apartheid.

And just as racism is a powerful myth, so is patriarchy, the notion that males should dominate females as a matter of course. And this obviously does not only apply to white males, but to all males, not least in our society which is riddled with violence against women as much in the townships as in the suburbs. It has taken a long while for males to recognize the injustice of the patriarchal myth even in sophisticated European countries. After all, women only got the vote in Switzerland after the Second World War—and Switzerland prides itself on being a modern society and model for democracy! Just like racism, patriarchy is a social construction of reality. And for males to change that reality it has to be deconstructed, and males should be engaged in doing that just as they must be engaged in combatting racism. But can we break the genetic code that makes us white males?

CAN WE BREAK THE GENETIC CODE?

Yes, conversions do happen, and the conversion of St. Paul on the Damascus Road is the paradigmatic example most quoted. However, remember this, the narrative of Paul's conversion was not about how he got to heaven, but how he received new sight and became a changed man. The story is all about a privileged Pharisee and persecutor of despised Christians outside the pale of decent society, became an apostle who ended up serving them at great cost to himself. How a bigoted racist and religionist, as well as a male chauvinist, became someone who proclaimed an inclusive gospel which embraced everyone whether they were slaves or freemen, whether they were Jews or Gentiles, whether they were male or female. The persecutor and misogynist entered the kingdom of God because God took him by the scruff of his neck and with the help of a few friends he was given a new set of eyes with which to see reality, and a new set of ears which enabled him to hear differently. But more than that, he not only heard and saw differently he had the courage to act differently. To break the rules that were unjust, unfair and kept others in bondage. And in doing so Paul discovered who he was truly meant to be, free from the bondages of the past.

So, can a white male change his genetic code and enter the kingdom of heaven? Or is not everything determined by ancestry and genes?

Many of Steve's ancestors were Vikings, knights, crusaders and one was a one general. His great-grandparents were British settlers and colonists. So how was it that Steve the descendant of war-like macho Vikings became a pacifist, conscientious objector and advocate of gender equality, and how come that he, the descendants of colonialists, was a proponent of post-colonialism? How did this white male South African buck the trend that his genes dictated and made a valiant attempt to enter the kingdom of God?

Virtually from the day he was born, Steve had his own mind. He may have been baptized Stephen, but he decided to be Steve. He did not play rugby and cricket; he played soccer and the guitar. He befriended strangers. He had black friends and gay friends. In addition, he became a conscientious objector; refusing be part of the system. Moreover, he was not alone. Like other courageous young white South African males who undermined the dominant white male paradigm, he too broke the stereotype of their tribe and class. They began to see things, as Bonhoeffer once said, "from below", from the perspective of the less privileged and the oppressed. They decided not to follow the crowd of white male South Africans, but rather to seek first God's kingdom of justice and peace. It was difficult, very difficult at times, but not impossible, and the temptation to walk away was always present.

Steve Biko not only taught us that blacks had to liberate themselves; he also said they had to help whites liberate themselves and that when whites are liberated, they become black! By that he meant there were whites who had somehow broken free or been liberated from their "whiteness" by joining in the struggle against apartheid. Among them were people like Ds. Beyers Naude and Advocate Braam Fischer and those brave white women who led the Black Sash. They had consciously broken free from the captivity of their whiteness, at least as far as that was possible.

The question, then, is not *can* a white male South African enter the kingdom of God, but *how* can he do so? If the first step towards white male liberation requires acknowledging guilt for the sins we have perpetrated, rather than feeling sorry for ourselves, making excuses, denying reality, looking for ways to escape, the second is getting rid of the idea that we cannot change, that we are who we are by birth and there is nothing more to be said. But that this is a fallacy is obvious because some have broken free, refused to conform to the patterns imposed by the dominant and prevailing norms and skewed values of society. And Steve was one of them.

THE ROLE OF MENTORS AND COMMUNITIES

Looking back over the years to the time when Steve was growing up Isobel and I can clearly see how it was that Steve became who he was. I do not mean how he became "perfect", a model son and a pious Christian. Steve was anything but a religious person as that word is normally understood. But he did decide to follow Christ, and in doing so he managed to break with norms that governed white apartheid society, as well as the norms that governed male patriarchal society. He also managed to break with the norms of a very homophobic and patriarchal society. But he did not do so alone in isolation from others. Steve had friends and mentors, and he belonged to communities and groups that enabled, encourage and empowered him. Who he became did not just happen overnight or in an instant. It was the outcome of a long process of formation.

Whatever influences there may have been in the family, one major factor was that Steve, as a member of this congregation, Rondebosch United, was exposed to an understanding of Christian faith that rejected apartheid and affirmed non-racialism. Steve's journey towards the kingdom heaven was enabled through the ministry of Douglas Bax and the youth ministry of Jim Cochrane. It is tragic that during the apartheid years far too many white churches reinforced racism rather than challenged it. Steve was blessed to be part of a Christian community that did the very opposite, and without that he would never have become who he became. Yes, of course, us Christians will say that transformation is the work of the Spirit in the life of an individual, but the Spirit works through human agency. And above all through communities of committed people who, from one generation to the next, pass on the values, hopes and skills that help people see things differently, break with the dominant norms of unjust, racist and patriarchal societies, and enter God's kingdom of justice. No one changes unless parents, mothers, mentors, colleagues, companions and congregations help make that happen.

Also important in Steve's journey towards the kingdom was his exposure to the teaching of the Bible in a way that not only made sense but also offered an alternative understanding of who he was and what it means to be a Christian living fully in the world. You are not going to break with white, male privilege if you read the Bible in ways that reinforce that understanding. So, you also need good teachers who help you understand what it means to be a Christian and a human being. You also need Christian mentors and icons who embody that different way of being Christian in the world. Icons such as those who influenced Steve -- Martin Luther King Jnr., Bonhoeffer, Beyers Naude, Desmond Tutu and Joe Wing. All of them were models that played a role in shaping Steve's changing consciousness. So did Steve's exposure when, on a sabbatical with us in the US, to the peace-witness of Mennonite Christians. And his involvement in the Student Union for Christian Action, and the wider life of a denomination that was a majority black church.

There was also his experience of young black Christians who both befriended and challenged him. as did those who were his companions on the "journey of hope" initiated by Archbishop Tutu, which took Steve to Taizé Community in France where he had his call to the ministry.

But it is often if not only when we hear the truth from the victims of oppression, only when we hear their stories and begin to participate with them in their struggles, that we actually begin to change. White South Africans cannot change in isolation from black South Africans. You cannot become a champion of justice if you are not enabled to see injustice through the eyes of those who experience it; you cannot become a worker for liberation if you do not experience something of the pain of oppression. You cannot really hear the gospel in a life-changing way if you only hear it from white voices. You cannot overcome fear of the other if you never meet and come to know the other.

And, of undoubted importance were youth training programmes that expose young white male South Africans to their black compatriots and do so on an equal footing, including the Volmoed Youth Leadership Training Programme to which we are inviting you this evening to contribute if you wish.

THE NEXT GENERATION

In closing I dedicate this lecture to David de Gruchy, Steve's son and my grandson, as a representative of a new generation of hopeful white South African males who love our country and are already making a contribution to the shaping of a better, more just, compassionate and sustainable South Africa. There are lots of them, young, white male South Africans willing to engage in shaping a better future, and willing to share what they have received for the benefit of us all. This is a sign of hope, for it is so easy to give up, to resign to fate, to fear for the future, and therefore to lose hope – especially if you feel you are, like the white rhino, part of an endangered species. But we all can make a difference, and in the process become better human beings. For in the end it does not matter whether we are white or black, male or female, South African or from elsewhere. What matters is that we are human beings with God-given capacity and gifts to use for the common good of our planet, and in the process also become better human beings.

"To those who have been given much," Jesus said, "much will be required." Most, if not all of us here this evening, have been given much. If we hope for a better future, a better South Africa, we have to turn the assets of privilege into authentic acts of hopefulness that make a difference not just to the lives of others, but also set us free to be more truly and fully who we are meant to be. Can a white male South African enter the kingdom of heaven? Yes, we can by the grace of God and with some help from our companions on the journey.

End of Lecture!

---

1. {Niebuhr :67}
2. {Barth 1981:164-5}

CHAPTER NINE

Artist, Ronald Harrison caused controversy in 1962 when he painted African National Congress (ANC) leader, Albert Luthuli as Jesus. The painting, named Black Christ, depicts Luthuli crucified on the cross next to apartheid mastermind Hendrik Verwoerd and former Minister of Justice John Vorster, who are depicted as Roman Soldiers. The painting not only challenged the apartheid system, but also the notion that Jesus was white. Harrison was arrested and the painting banned. The painting was smuggled to the United Kingdom and was only returned in 1997. Harrison died of cancer on 28 June 2011, just before he was to exhibit his latest work. Black Christ remains his most famous work. The painting is now housed at the South African National Gallery.

Wilhelm Verwoerd, whom I consider a friend, is a slender tallish chap who has a reluctant smile. His seriousness about justice and reconciliation can be seen in his countenance. Wilhelm certainly does feel the burden of carrying the Verwoerd name. He has had deep conversations about the

"Black Christ" painting and how his grandfather was depicted in the painting. I met him during some of his conversations around the painting and was quite taken by his sincerity, making himself vulnerable. One can easily think that Wilhelm is a saint, something that his lovely wife Sharon, may dispute! Wilhelm has recently published a book with the title: *"My Journey through Family Betrayals"*.

In this book he tells the stories of his own journey from uncritically accepting the racist political ideology of his grandfather, and eventually choosing instead to commit to social justice. He has also shared his story of becoming a member of the ANC in public platforms, campaigning for the party in 1994, working for the Truth and Reconciliation Commission, and spending a large part of his adult life doing reconciliation work across the globe, including here in South Africa and Ireland.

Wilhelm was present when De Gruchy gave the memorial lecture in honour of his son. Below is Wilhelm's response.

WILHELM VERWOERD'S RESPONSE

I am honoured and humbled to have this opportunity to respond to John's lecture. I am still vibrating, like a light-brown Tibetan singing bowl, from a 6-hour comrade's marathon on Easter Sunday (21 April). I joined my neighbour family, the Mabebas, and thousands of black South Africans in white clothes in an unused warehouse near the airport, led by Apostle Mohlala of Shekinah Healing Ministries. I mostly basked in the vibrancy of their embodied, rather loud singing and praying. So, it feels right, despite my much greater comfort with contemplative spirituality, to start my response with a loud "Amen!" And an even more enthusiastic "Hallelujah!!"

Thank God for someone like Steve De Gruchy. Thank you, John, Isobel and all the mentors from across historical divides for your vital contributions to Steve's all too short life. Thank you, John, for also being an embodied signpost for white, male South Africans trying to enter the nearby heaven, at this time, on this piece of Mother Earth.

A PERSONALIZED RESPONSE:

I mean what I say. Even though you are English-speaking! Thank you for inviting me to give this response. It is another step on my Afrikaner journey of deep reconciliation with English-speaking white South Africans.

On this note I would like to express my gratitude to a close colleague from Steve's "tribe" who helped him come a bit more alive for me. Theresa Edlmann shared the following vivid memory as I prepared this response: "We were at a SUCA (Students' Union for Christian Action) congress, at Katberg in the Eastern Cape, in December 1984. There were busloads and carloads of people who came from all corners of the country – from Turfloop, MEDUNSA, Jo'burg, University of Zululand, the Natal universities, UCT, Stellenbosch, UPE, Rhodes. There was a lot of discussion about what was happening in the country, including the recent establishment of the ECC (End Conscription Campaign).

There was this white guy sitting in the back – he was the bus driver for the Stellenbosch delegation and was kind of included in the conference. It was clear that he was getting increasingly angry as he listened to speaker after speaker. At one stage he stormed to the front, took off his sunhat, threw it on the front desk and said in Afrikaans, 'Julle mense praat 'n klomp K**K!' (You people are talking a lot of sh*t!) And then went into this long tirade about how furious all this stuff from black people and English-speaking liberal people were making him, concluding with a passionate justification of apartheid. The majority of this congress of well over a hundred people sat in stunned silence, including myself.

The one person who instantly moved to the front and embraced this man was Steve De Gruchy. Steve then stepped in and facilitated this extraordinarily compassionate response to this man and invited a dialogue between him and members of the congress. This symbolised for me everything that Steve at his best was."

I wish I was part of SUCA! Actually, in 1984 I was chair of the lilywhite "Admissiebond" (Dutch Reformed Church, undergraduate theology students' society). To my shame, like the bus driver, I was still cheering on the army and the police's "holy war" against the "total onslaught" of "ANC Communists and terrorists".

Without straying too far from John's focus, let me say that a part of me is grateful for the careful limitation of John's question. If he included ethnicity, sexual orientation, class and family the ashamed parts of me would have been even more tempted to run away from the question on the table. For a personalised, intersectional framing of the question would read something like: Can I, a white, male, heterosexual, middle class, middle-aged, Afrikaans-speaking, Dutch Reformed Church, Stellenbosch, Verwoerd, enter the kingdom of heaven?!

The bottom line is that each of these entangled parts of my South African self represents large scale pain of one or other "Them" given the systemic privileging of "Us" and abuse of power by "Us". Untangling this kraaines often feels impossible. However, thanks to the heavenly truth embodied in genuine Ubuntu, the mediated good news for me is that the path to "heaven" – to the ultimate reality of radically inclusive interconnectedness - is more or less the same for each strand of my current South African socio-political identity.

Ironically, it is in facing the most troubling and troubled part of who I am – the patriarchal-whiteness-with-vuma genes in my blood – that a number of South Africans of colour gifted me a deceptively simple key to the gates of heaven. Often, I've been assured by people such as Pumla Gobodo-Madikizela, Themba Lonzi, Theo Mayekiso and Spiwo Xapile that "we are not asking you to reject your grandfather, in our culture we respect our ancestors. The real question is what are you willing to do, with us, to address the apartheid legacies of Verwoerd?" When I asked Archbishop Tutu's guidance during my most recent attempt to come home more deeply in my kin and my skin, his open-armed fatherly advice was: "don't run away from who you are, use the power of your name for good…".[1]

In other words, do not run away from the pain associated with the Architect of Apartheid, use the inherited symbolic power of your surname to help transform the pain of ongoing, dehumanizing divisions.

Through the undeserved midwifery of many other people (including Zanele Khumalo, Marcella Naidoo, Kevin Patel, Edwin Arrison, and Dudley and Ashnat Adolph) I've come to understand that, humanly speaking, there is indeed a liberating, affirmative answer to even the fleshed out version of John's question:

Acknowledge the (historical and ongoing) **pain** caused and represented by each part of my socio-political identity.

Then use the **privilege** and **power** associated with each of these parts to contribute, humbly, to the transformation of this (visible and invisible) pain.

AN URGENT CALL TO WHITE WORK

I wish I knew Steve, but from what I have gathered again in John's lecture and from Theresa's anecdote, he embodied the above kind of answer. And to the extent that Steve did, he entered heaven before his tragic bodily death. Which brings me to the burning question behind the disturbing title of John's memorial lecture, a question raised with increasing intensity by young, post-1994 black South Africans: why are so few of us that look like Steve following in his steps? Why is it necessary for John to pose his question 25 years after our first democratic election?

I see John's question and answer and my response mainly as contributions to urgently needed "white work". At a public conversation last Friday, April 26th, at the Suidoosterfees, Haji Mohamed Dawjee stressed again that it is high time for white South Africans to stop expecting people of colour to "move on" and to rather do some serious self-reflection amongst themselves about what it really means to be a white South African today. For the last few years, I have taken seriously this kind of challenge to people that look like me to increase self-critical historical awareness, in preparation for real racial transformation. So, thank you for posing your deep-water question, John.

I do share John's caution about making generalising statements about "white male South Africans". And I agree that, on the other hand, we must make the ongoing legacies of systematic privileging based on skin colour more visible. For it seems to me that not only was Steve part of small white minority opposing patriarchal white rule during his lifetime, but the same can be said of his son David in post-1994 South Africa given what John shared about David's willingness to accept the responsibility that comes with inherited racialized power and privileges. I would love to meet David and hear more about his journey.

I am deeply concerned about the lack of historical awareness that I encounter in white circles, especially amongst younger generations. I often wish that the TRC had a wider mandate to help generate an abiding, creative awareness of the systemic dehumanization of apartheid and colonialism! Perhaps it is not too late for a nation-wide, community-based Truth and Responsibility Commission of this kind? In the meantime, white Christians who want to enter heaven in South Africa may further our urgent (re)education by taking to heart these historical reasons why "political supremacy and racial capitalism impoverished Africans and enriched whites undeservedly" (as late Economics Prof. Sampie Terreblance put it at the TRC Business Sector hearing in 1997):

Firstly, the Africans were deprived of a large part of land on which they conducted successful traditional farming for centuries. White farmers on the other hand had the privilege of property rights and access to very cheap and docile African labour, my father included.

Secondly, for decades, millions of Africans were paid exploitative wages, in all sectors of the economy but mainly in gold mining and agriculture.

Thirdly, a great variety of discriminative legislation not only deprived Africans of the opportunity to acquire skills, but also compelled and humiliated them to do really unskilled work at very low wages.

Fourthly, perhaps the greatest disadvantage which the prevailing power structures had for Africans is that these structures deprived them of opportunities to accumulate human capital, the most important form of capital in the twentieth century. For the first three quarters of the century, social spending, on education, pensions etcetera, on Africans, was per capita, more or less ten to eight times smaller than on whites. In 1970, the per capita spending on white education was twenty times higher than the per capita spending on Africans.

Fifthly, the fact that a legal right to own property and to conduct a business was strongly restricted in the case of Africans also deprived them of the opportunity to accumulate property and to develop entrepreneurial and professional capabilities. The position of whites was again the complete opposite.

(TRC Report, Vol. V, Ch. 9, pp. 409-10)

The huge facilitation challenge is to translate this kind of (conveniently neglected) painful information about the ABC of Apartheid into visible and invisible transformation, into actions and attitudes of sustainable restitution.

Without this restitutional translation, people like me also become complicit in undermining the memory of people like Steve and many others who sacrificed so much to make the political transition in 1994 possible. One of the most disturbing aspects of our current Fallist context is the questioning of people like former pres. Mandela and Archbishop Tutu for not being radical enough.

My sense is that a major contributing factor is unjustly privileged white South Africans' all too comfortable embrace of a grandfatherly "Madiba" and a smiling "Arch", accepting their costly, undeserved welcoming of people like me as fellow sons and daughters of South Africa (Luthuli), without facing the painful meaning of whiteness and without taking shared responsibility for the pervasive dehumanizing legacies of colonialism and Apartheid.

I suspect that is why a part of me felt quite uncomfortable to also wear a white shirt during that joyful Easter Sunday celebration at Shekinah Healing Ministries. Yes, I accept that in many church circles white is used as a symbol of light and new life. And I was warmly welcomed with my white shirt despite the heavy baggage of my "colourless" skin. Indeed, an encouraging taste of heaven. But on the way to and from church we drove through Driftsands "informal settlement", passing Mfuleni and Khayelitsha - stark reminders of racialized poverty, of skin-linked inequality which did not drop from the sky as pointed out again by Prof. Sampie.

The troubling question haunting me with renewed intensity after Easter is this: how many white South African Christians have embraced the (pre-Zuma) "new South Africa" as if it is possible really to celebrate Easter Sunday without participating in the preceding period of lent and especially Good Friday? How many of us – me included - like to put on the equivalents of uplifting white spiritual clothes, without facing the darkness and death represented by whiteness, without daily taking up our historical cross as unjustly privileged white South Africans?

This variation on John's question might be helpful as a provocative diagnosis of a central root of increasing racial tensions in a post-1994 South Africa where the language of "post-apartheid" increasingly rings hollow and the murky state capture political waters tend to blur our founding non-racial vision. The urgent follow-on question is: HOW can many more (old and young) white South Africans really follow (the historical) Jesus?[2]

How do people like me pause our confident, fashionable finger-pointing at Zuma and co in present-day South Africa to make sure that our cushy critique of black corruption is not another form of running away from our shared historical responsibility for a crime against humanity? How do people like me (and our children) descend into and journey through the hell of separateness (from self, others and God) as the only path to greater awareness of the "kingdom"[3] of heaven, in South Africa, today?

A VOLMOED TASTE

I am particularly grateful that John addressed this HOW question in an embodied way, by giving us a glimpse of Steve's journeying through apartheid, facilitated by family, friends and church communities across political illusions of human separateness.

In similar vein I want to refer to a life histories workshop at Volmoed in June 2018, which I was privileged to facilitate with Themba Lonzi and Zanele Khumalo. I experienced this open-hearted three-day journey with an ecumenical, diverse group of Church Youth Leaders, including three young (white male) NGK dominees, as a gentle, all too fleeting touch of the kingdom of heaven.

I am, of course, not referring to a fake news, white-washed "rainbow-ism" which cannot be reconciled with Archbishop

Tutu's profound kingdom vision of a "rainbow nation of God" in the midst of our dehumanizing divisions. We spend a good bit of time creating a working agreement on how to be honest and real with each other given the very different histories present in the room. We regularly drummed together. Making wonky but enjoyable "organized noise" with drums of different shapes and sizes, despite our different abilities to follow's Themba's lead, encouraged more trust in the process. So did eating together in a beautiful environment without the usual distractions.

Most of the time we sat in large and small circles listening deeply to often painful life experiences, each person getting an unrushed, uninterrupted opportunity to share what they feel ready to share. On the second evening we ended up sitting tightly around the fire-pit in the lapa area. It was a clear, crisp winter's evening. We prayed and sang and laughed together. As the hallelujah refrain of Ukuthula soared into the black sky, accompanied by the Ubuntu rhythms of Themba's drum, a deep sense of homecoming surfaced. In this colourful circle. And in my tainted skin.

I was not alone in sensing that something infinitely precious, transcending language, happened amongst us at Volmoed. Feedback from some of the women of colour included "this is the first time that I saw a white man being vulnerable, it meant a lot to me"; one NGK *dominee* said afterwards: "these few days gave me a taste of non-racialism, and the taste was delicious".

There is so much more to say about the promise, the process and the pitfalls of this kind of humanization journey.[4] Given John's focus I want to zoom in a bit on the preparatory and follow-up "white work" with those three NGK dominees who were part of this Volmoed process.

In early 2018 Theresa Edlmann, and I were invited to accompany a dozen or so young NGK dominees in their desire to promote restitutional racial healing, despite resistance from some older congregants. They accepted our encouragement that as facilitators we cannot ask people to go to places that we are not willing to go ourselves. Our first step therefore became a three day deep-dive into how each of us have been shaped in our "whiteness" as South Africans – exploring childhoods and family lives, as well as living and working in environments that typically are still largely white.

We drew on Alan Storey's example of daring to be prophetic, without becoming unloving or holier than thou. We discussed how we can support each other on what often feels like a lonely, frustrating path of trying to remain true to our faith, especially amongst (older) family and ethnic kin. And even more if you are one of the few young female dominees. We started to make individual and collective plans to take the next steps of engaging with South Africans of colour, while giving up our need for control.

One of these steps was to accept Edwin Arrison's invitation for a few members of this group to participate in the Reconciliation Week of the Volmoed Church Youth Leaders Programme. My sense is that their first phase of white work was indeed good preparation. From my point of view this kind of "intragroup" process contributed to the white dominees' ability to participate with more self-aware humility and an empowered restitutional attitude in the above Volmoed journey.

We are continuing to develop the white work strand together, including intergenerational dialogue with NGK church leadership as initial representatives of the sanctified sins of (white Afrikaner) fathers.

In the process two major obstacles on the road to the kingdom of heaven have so far come to the fore. The first underlines how exceptional Steve De Gruchy was in becoming a conscientious objector during a time of white male conscription.

MILITARIZED WHITE MASCULINITY

I do appreciate someone with John's anti-apartheid political pedigree drawing attention to the negative consequences for many white men who were conscripted into fighting the "Border War" or doing their compulsory "military service" in the townships.

This is clearly not about minimizing the much wider destructive impacts of these men's actions on black communities in South Africa and neighboring countries. But white work has to include an explicit grappling with the gendered and intergenerational impacts of militarized white masculinity, with the "lingering unspoken pain of white youth who fought for apartheid"[5].

Demilitarizing white work will, however, have to take into account the different, culturally specific journeys of change of someone like Steve and someone like myself. I was moved by John's pride in Steve's faith-based opposition to apartheid and in his warmth towards David's embrace of being a young white South African male.

I assume these feelings were and are mutual. Listening to a number of the young Afrikaans-speaking NGK dominees struggling with their fathers' defensiveness regarding the previous regime, with these fathers' unwillingness to talk about or to question what they literally fought for, I recognized my own struggles with my father and my grandfather (and the mainstream fathers of the NGK and the volk). Yes, there are enduring strands of loyalty and love. But anger, shame and being accused of betrayal when voicing the shame featured more prominently, especially in my 20s and 30s.

I remain particularly interested in how to transform these kinds of intergenerational dynamics in which potentially destructive moral emotions of guilt and shame feature prominently. The temptation to run away from who I am has a lot to do, I've found, with the embodied, almost instinctive desire to hide from what I and many of the groups I'm connected with have done to other people. Resisting this desire requires more than conventional PTSD therapy, or storytelling workshops.

At stake is the profound spiritual challenge of recovering from "moral injury"[6] – a wounding of the soul through involvement in something that goes against your deepest values. The urgent question is, where do white (Afrikaner) veterans go to find spiritual guidance through this "dark night of the soul"?

There is of course the possibility that these troubled intergenerational dynamics are not so unique to militarized white Afrikaner Christians. I would love to hear more from, for example, John and David about the emotional and spiritual complexity of their relationships with the British settlers in their genealogy. Are they also struggling with the shame of family associations with colonialism, another crime against the kingdom of God? And more broadly, does the Western liberal tradition's cherishing of individual freedom make English-speaking white South Africans particularly prone to running away from shared historical responsibility?

I am grateful that John highlighted the need for all white South Africans to identify with the younger brother in the Parable of the Prodigal Son: we need to resist running away and face our historical shame if we want to return home to our Father and Mother's kingdom.

However, the older brother is also part of our white story. This brings me to the second, less visible obstacle mentioned above.

WHITE PATERNALISM

In listening to the childhood experiences of a younger generation of white (Afrikaans-speaking) South Africans, I was struck and disturbed by how similar our early socialization has been. Our primary exposure to South Africans of colour was in the context of unequal, paternalistic relations with domestic workers and child minders.

A major problem with this kind of paternalistic (or materialistic) socialization and the overall perception of myself as a "good white" is the continuing reluctance fully to accept Biko's critique of "white liberals".

Instead of thoroughly examining the falseness of my inherited sense of superiority and uprooting my ingrained tendencies to control and prescribe, I easily become self-righteous and indignant when faced with criticisms of racism: "I care about justice and inequality.

I treat my domestic worker well; I even pay for the education of her child. I am NOT a racist!" In other words, I start to behave like the older brother in the parable of the prodigal son. The problem is that it is much more difficult for "good people" truly to return home, as pointed out by Henri Nouwen:

"The lostness of the elder son is much harder to identify... The lostness of the resentful 'saint' is so hard to reach precisely because it is so closely welded to the desire to be good and virtuous … Returning home from a lustful escapade seems so much easier than returning home from a cold anger that has rooted itself in the deepest corners of my being."[7]

HOMECOMING

Can a white male South African enter the kingdom of heaven? Can I come home in a relational, purified-ubuntu quality of being that includes and transcends all visible, earthly distinctions of kin and skin?

At the individual, interpersonal level, I want to answer yes. I have tasted this possibility a few times. And it was too delicious for words. However, the haunting of the dehumanising shadow of separateness remains pervasive and often feels overwhelming.

It is very significant for me that the Centre hosted John's lecture for Christian Spirituality. Through this Centre I became exposed in the early 1990s to Anthony De Mello, Thomas Keating, Richard Rohr and John O'Donohue.[8] Since then a committed contemplative spiritual practice has become indispensable in not running away from who I am and what I represent in South Africa.

I have gradually been enabled, through God's grace and the Body of Christ, to accept being born into a particular family and skin and place and time as an invitation to participate in the life-giving mystery of the Incarnation.[9] This mystery includes a daily, embodied carrying of my cross, as I was reminded again a week ago on Easter Sunday. Returning from the colourful service we not only drove past stark reminders of racialized poverty. I also went to visit my elderly parents in their white, middle class neighbourhood of Stellenbosch.

In the hallway, a large portrait of Oupa Hendrik greeted me again. The temptation was intense to close the door of my heart, to give up trying to hold on to these opposing worlds. But then I felt my arms being held up by my Mabeba neighbours, mama Emily and sister Naledi. And Sheikh Ismail Keraan from District Six. I also remembered people like Pumla and Theresa and Themba's encouragements. I felt Father Tutu's warm embrace. And I heard the cheers of many ancestors, including Chief Luthuli, oom Bey and brother Steve De Gruchy.

---

1. See *Verwoerd: My journey through family betrayals*, Tafelberg, 2019.
2. Marcus Borg's *Meeting Jesus again for the first time: The historical Jesus and the heart of contemporary faith* (Harper Collins, 1994) continues to be very helpful to me in this regard.
3. I first encountered this variation in Paul Knitter's inspiring *Without Buddha I could not be a Christian*. In a footnote on p. 93 he writes "To avoid the patriarchal tones of 'Kingdom' I'm following the advice of feminist theologians who suggest this neologism as being closer to the familial society of love and justice that Jesus intended." I love the non-exclusionary, truly Christian vision of a "kingdom" – a family-without-any- human-made-boundaries. For me it has become critical to understand that membership of this family is based on the "original blessing" (Matthew Fox) of being created, like ALL other people, in the "image and likeness of God" (Gen. 3), given the traces of exclusionary Calvinist predestination in my theological bones. I am leaving aside for the moment the Franciscan ecological inclusion of, for example, "Brother" Son and "Sister" Moon. For my participation in a small attempt to bring this "soul, soil and society" (Satish Kumar) kingdom down to earth, see Lynedoch Ecovillage at www.sustainabili-tyinstitute.net.
4. See Alistair Little and Wilhelm Verwoerd, *Journey through Conflict Trail Guide: Introduction* (Trafford, 2013)
5. See Theresa Edlmann's article in *The Conversation* (which has received more than a million viewings since publication!) https://theconversation.com/the-lingering-unspoken-pain-of-white-youth-who-fought-for-apartheid-46218
6. See Robert Meagher's *Killing from the Inside Out: Moral Injury and Just War* (Cascade Books, 2014).
7. *Return of the Prodigal Son*, pp. 70, 82

8. I've treasured the "meaningful co-incidence" (Jung) of preparing my response to John's question during a two week period when Richard Rohr's Daily Meditations (including contributions by James Finley and Cynthia Bourgeault) dealt with the theme of "Heaven". The highly relevant archive is available at the Centre for Action and Contemplation's extremely helpful website: www.cac.org.

9. On another occasion I would love to expand much more on an emerging, embodied spirituality of deep reconciliation that is the taproot of my life.

PART THREE

Social Restitution: A Journey

CHAPTER TEN

M y interest in this topic is because of my involvement on issues of justice, peace and reconciliation in South Africa, particularly in the City of Cape Town, where I have worked with many church denominations and parts of civil society that have wrestled with this issue. I, together with many fellow pilgrims and compatriots, have even travelled to countries in South America in our quest to find a model that we could work with in South Africa to bring about lasting peace in our country.

In the year 2002, a few of us gathered in a house in Cape Town, at the invitation of Charles Robertson, and deliberated about this issue. This resulted in many conversations that led to the formation of the Restitution Foundation (RF), which consisted of white, coloured and black compatriots. I chaired the Foundation, until I decided to pursue other interests in another province hoping that the RF would make a significant impact in South Africa and be able to address the injustices and inequalities of the past directly linked to an unjust system of apartheid and oppression.

During my absence, the RF embarked on a mission in Worcester to implement a programme of peace, justice, reconciliation, and restitution. It has now been seven years since this mission was embarked upon and, I have been approached to lend a helping hand again to assist in the process of bringing lasting peace that is based on restitution in the town of Worcester.

The hope is that this becomes a model for the New South Africa. I am personally sold on the idea of being a co-creator of a better South Africa with genuine peace, reconciliation, and restitution. I believe that South Africa belongs to all who live in it, and that hurts and deprivation of the past policies of apartheid cannot be simple glossed over. There must be a concerted effort on the part of civil society to be agents of transformation and shapers of the future.

South Africa has a turbulent past as a result of the discriminatory policies of the apartheid state. The new political dispensation in 1994 brought about renewed hope for a better country where racism would be outdated and where poverty and strife would have been relegated to the dustbin of history. There was hope and belief that the era of President Nelson Mandela would bring to an end the divisions and pain of the past, through The Truth and Reconciliation Commission (TRC) that would address the injustices of the past by encouraging the perpetrators to come forward, and confess in order to receive pardon.

The victims of the brutality of apartheid were to receive compensation for their suffering and loss. This good foundation would lead to greatness as a country that is at peace with itself and at peace with the world. The international community promptly embraced the new nation and opened its doors by lifting economic sanctions and trade embargoes. The new South Africa was admired and declared a model for reconciliation, peace and justice.

However, many South Africans soon realized that it was not to be. Divisions between the races continued unabated. The gap between the rich and poor continued to grow. Some of the victims of past injustices never received reparations or compensation; in fact, it was made clear from the start that the victims of apartheid should expect little from the TRC process. Currently, questions are being asked about the role of the TRC and whether it did in fact bring reconciliation, peace and justice in South Africa.

It is into this context that the Worcester Hope and Reconciliation Process (WHRP) was founded. This was an initiative of the Restitution Foundation that sought to address some of the issues of reconciliation through restitution. Restitution, according to Professor Sharlene Swartz, the current chairperson of the RF is a difficult word to describe, but can be summed up as something that is about bringing a matter to its former state before an injustice was done. Perhaps it could be described as 'going beyond reconciliation - repentance and just being 'sorry' .

It is a process where the beneficiaries of the past injustices acknowledge that they have benefited because of an unfair system and begin to take steps towards 'making right' by doing restitution actions of paying back through different means.

Worcester was chosen because of its unique history in terms of incidences of racial oppression and also, its size, which is neither too big nor too small. More importantly, because there was a bombing incident that took place on Christmas Eve in 1996 by a South African anti state group called The Boere Aanvals Troepe.

The first task of the WHRP was to bring the perpetrators of the so-called 'Worcester Bombings' together with the victims of the terrorism. The victims were members of the Khulumani organization whose main purpose is to find the victims of apartheid brutality and assist them in their quest for justice. The victims of the bombings were coloured and black residents of Worcester whereas the perpetrators were white Afrikaners who belonged to a right-wing movement.

The WHRP was able to successfully bring the bomb survivors to meet one of the perpetrators who was in prison at the time some 1300 km away.

The bomb survivors travelled by train, dubbed the peace train, for the sole purpose of being part of a reconciliation act. This moving ceremony gripped the town, and attracted the attention of many and as a result, there was some enthusiasm generated in the town for reconciliation and restitution. Certain events started taking place in the town such as the "Koinonia Meals" where members of different race groups would come together for conversations that matter. The major stakeholders in this process were Khulumani members who represented black and coloured residents of Worcester, as well as the Dutch Reformed Church (DRC) and some of their followers who represented mainly the white Afrikaner residents of Worcester. It is important to note that the white members of WHRP were not exclusively Afrikaans and not exclusively churchgoers.

This initiative with the WHRP has been going on since 2002 when a few people that were concerned about the country and its future gathered to commit to this process.

South Africa remains a country where there is a massive gap between the poor and the rich. This gap is according to race and is clearly an outcome of South Africa's past racist policies.

This has had a negative effect on the population. Some success has been achieved in South Africa in terms of race relations between black and white South Africans but more progress is needed and the narrow understanding of reconciliation by many white South Africans must be overcome.

This history is causing irreversible harm to the next generation and cannot be simply ignored. For example, Reynolds refers to the young people of Worcester as militarized because of abject poverty and inhuman conditions. Snyman writes about socio economic justice that has not become a reality in Worcester and that goes for many other towns and cities in South Africa.

Socio-economic justice would require a new paradigm in terms of how people of this nation see themselves and what changes are necessary at a personal level. Historically, there have been examples of scholars who have wrestled with the phenomenon of injustice and who try to offer some solutions, such as Spivak, who calls for a 'transformation of consciousness—a changing mind set' (Sanders, 2006:62). For Spivak there must be a shift in the mind set. Paradigm shift, one might say, away from naïve consciousness.

Fanon calls for a 'decolonization' (Newlove, 2017). This would mean to have a mind that is not influenced by colonial projects. Freire calls for 'conscientization' (Lloyd, 1972), a great believer in synergy between spirituality and development. Haraway calls for 'accountable positioning' (Haraway, 1988). An interpretation of this could mean that because of our historical positioning in terms of gender (patriarchy) or race (white supremacy), we must consciously reposition ourselves. There is therefore a need to delve deeply into the issues of justice, reconciliation and restitution in nation building and social cohesion. A mechanism that can assist the process to make the dream of social cohesion, sustainable peace, social restitution, and sustainable development a reality is required.

PART FOUR

"Voices from Worcester"

CHAPTER ELEVEN

Gibson, a well-respected member of the process, and a church leader in Worcester for many years, has made numerous attempts to reach out to other races and explains that this is very important work that other members of the white community ought to be doing. He states that:

It is necessary. I think from a white perspective it is not just about money; it has to restore dignity. To real how the past has wounded all of us. I understand people's fears and anger. People just want this to go away. They will avoid it, and some are too angry to talk about it. They have just closed their eyes and do not want to think about it. They bury their heads in the ground. What might be asked? We have become shallow and not thoughtful – escaping to stay shallow. As a community, we have resorted to living shallow from day to day. People don't want to think deeply, so they rather avoid. It costs more than some are prepared to give. There are many reasons.

Gibson sounded troubled and deeply affected by the way things are and that his fellow white compatriots seem to have chosen a back seat.

Suzanne also expresses a similar sentiment regarding conversations. She recalls the days of the struggle and as a white liberal, was aware of what was happening in the black and coloured communities where street committees were formed, as she states the following:

> ... The community of Worcester needs to get together street committees. Get people to talk with input from everyone. It should start with conversation.

It was also said in the interview that perhaps these conversations would have to be facilitated and managed in such a way that they don't lose focus or divide the community further.

There was also a feeling that these conversations must start at home with family and relatives, even though this may be difficult in some contexts. Lydia, who lives in a coloured neighborhood with her parents, was able to have conversation with her mother. Her mother seems to have experienced a lot of hardship under the previous regime. She goes on to say:

> My family, my mother and I talk a lot about it. She is over 80 and has been through apartheid. It is not easy to reconcile. It is still a struggle; apartheid is still very fresh.

The mother lost her brother. A white person was responsible and nothing happened. The first thing is that we must express our feelings and get together. It is not easy, sometimes people don't want to hear the truth. Church is not active in reconciling. There is a need for dialogue.

It came up in the conversations repeatedly that Worcester is not alone in this and that the whole of South Africa is dealing with the same challenges. Perhaps the people of Worcester wanted to feel a bit better about themselves and not as if they are the only ones that are not getting things right? It could also have been a way of escapism and diverting focus away from them. This assertion came mostly from the white participants.

I think Suzanne would summarize her thoughts in this way:

I think the whole of SA needs restitution.

Different viewpoints

The privilege group wants cheap forgiveness.

One can't keep on forgiving if lives do not change.

They don't know the physical thing.

The participants expressed in so many ways that it is not easy to talk about restitution and that many people get offended when the subject comes up. One white participant mentioned that when she hears the word "restitution" the first thing that comes to her mind is "compensation", meaning that she owes someone something. She feels that the debt is too big and would not even know where to begin so its best not to use the word "restitution". There has even been the suggestion that another word must be found that would not sound "so bad or so confrontational."

Jacobus let go of some of his thoughts in this regard when he said the following:

> Look I have… I am one of those with guilty feelings… reaping the benefits of the previous state difficult to undo. When I was at the university, it hit me hard. Not sure, why it only started then. I met a coloured friend, Aubrey, who helped me see things differently, it was not accepted by others. I always look for God's way of answering private discussions. I am always a socialist, that is a better model. Difficult to let go of some of the benefits. You want your children to have the best. Some do not want to talk about it, some say let's fix it. You think about your children. Some are doing things to change stuff. I am not there yet.

It was easy to see that Jacobus was making himself very vulnerable as he wrestled with this question. He brings an interesting angle about being a socialist, which made me wonder about the relationship between social restitution and socialism. The question in this case would be whether social restitution is congruent with a capitalistic system. He mentions that he is aware of people who are at work trying to change things for the better. The issue of fear does come up as the children are mentioned and what their futures will look like.

The notion of 'safe spaces' has come up again; where people want to feel safe when they talk about issues of social justice and restitution. Being honest does make people feel vulnerable. However, Jacobus shared an interesting view that seems to differ from what his white friends think. He seems to think that safe spaces are important but is unsure about what the conversation or discussion ought to be about. He puts it as follows:

> I think it is critical that we must not create an environment where white males must ask for forgiveness. We must get past that. It happened, but how do we move forward. I get the view that some of my friends feel that they must ask for forgiveness.

I admire his honesty, but he clearly feels that something must be done, although he is not sure of what it must be. It is perhaps a good starting point. He then seems to answer his own question when he states the following:

> It's like how you change something. Change management philosophies start with the need for change. My experience with Aubrey opened my eyes around need for conversations. They play a big role.

I think it is healthy when people wrestle with these questions seeking an appropriate response. But they need to be encouraged.

Gibson, a respected white leader of the town, brought another angle to safe spaces. It would be easy to think of a 'safe space' just as a space to talk and voice out one's views, but Gibson takes it much further than a mere intellectual engagement that sometimes means very little. He emphatically states his point in the following sentence:

> If we cannot speak with one another, we struggle to hear the hearts of the people on the other side of town. So, we get our own images of those people living on the edges. I think we should take heart, and dare to put hearts on the table. It helps to create sate spaces, you get to hear something of their feelings, put something on the table.

Structural and cultural violence designed by the apartheid spatial planning has meant that people were not able to have spiritual connections with each other, unlike in metropolitan centres around the world. If we were not as separated geographically or spatially, the listening with the heart would lead to the connection of hearts where a new culture would evolve. This would be a Worcester culture and not a white, black or coloured culture.

Hilda mentioned at some stage that her classification as a coloured does not sit well with her. Many who are categorized as such share this. I have appreciated their understanding when I stated that changing the term could complicate this study a bit, as we are a nation still under construction. I suppose anti-racist training could lead to people respecting other cultures more.

Ali is a school principal and his school is a mix of coloured and black children mostly from the farms. It came naturally to him to talk about the education, having lived most of his life as an educator. He has his own bad experiences regarding discrimination and having been denied an opportunity to buy a house in the "right" part of town. He claims that the house that he could have bought 20 years ago for R70 000 is now worth R3 million and the house he ended up buying in the coloured area for the same amount is now worth a mere R500 000. "I will never catch up!" Ali says almost angrily. But then he quickly changes the subject and directs the conversation to the issues of education where there seems to be no change in terms of hiring teachers of colour. He is challenging things:

> "On a social basis in Worcester … I think like in the last principals' forum, I challenged then with one question. Found out how they feel… 70% is black and 95% is coloured. The staff is white… Why is there no change, two or three white teachers? The education system is not changing. The interns are white. The governing body is white. Land reform… a black lady I chatted with about land reform – farmers 50% must go to the workers… keep other so for food security. 70% of government is black and coloured

It appears from what Ali says that efforts are not being made to address the injustices in the workplace. The need for social justice or social restitution may not have permeated into the classrooms of Worcester.

This might be the reason why Hilda, who used to harbor fugitives' in her house and then send them to Umkhonto Wesizwe camps in exile, feels that people need education in a different sense. Hilda continues to be an activist, but now a social activist as opposed to being a political activist. People wonder why she is doing what she is doing. I asked her why and she responded:

> People ask me why I am so involved in the white people's things. Yes, it is a matter of education. People must know why. I think we cannot run from political activism. I am now more for social cohesion – people ask why I am supporting all the blacks. We still have division. I am trying hard to bring a united Worcester. My role is social cohesion."

Hilda will still have to work hard, it seems, because there is also a big chasm between coloureds and blacks in Worcester, although the two groups find common ground when it relates to white oppression and the injustices of the past that are still felt today. Some coloured people realize that as much as they suffered under an unjust system, they had a slight advantage over black people because of their proximity to whiteness, thus earning some extra privilege. Hilda seems to subscribe to that belief. She believes that she is an educator, albeit out of the classroom.

Olwethu, a Worcester bomb survivor who now believes that there must be financial commitment towards education for young people, says:

> To know if there is real change, they would have to make some financial commitment, especially in education for the next generation. Definitely, talking with and educating people. They must be honest conversations. No exclusion.

Olwethu's view is shared by many who believe that things should not just be about this generation. Conversations and discussion that take place should always take cognizance of the next generation. In other words, there has to be foresight because the future belongs to the next generation.

Several participants wanted to take the issue beyond just informal conversations at home and with friends and relatives; they say it should lead to formal discussions. This would be education in the form of workshops with qualified and skilled facilitators that help people unlearn inherited tendencies of discrimination and racial elitism. Some participants even alluded to the fact that people must be forced to take part in these discussion because of the value they could bring towards the co creation of a better town and better communities. One participant said that if he had the means he would hire a big hall, get everybody inside and not let them out until they come with answers. Suzanne put it this way:

> Worcester would have to sit down and discuss it, maybe set up a trust fund with a point system. For the (bomb) survivors maybe with education. I thought about that with the survivors, but that caused division.
>
> Maybe an emergency fund. It is very necessary to have honest talks. We must persuade people to talk about it. We are going to land in a bad situation. We should start by talking about it. It is a process that does not end. It must continue. People get hurt all the time. It's a process… a difficult process.

The participants expressed the need for, and even frustrations about the absence of practical examples of a community that is committed to reaching out to each other across the divides. But there is also support for conversations and dialogues that can cut across these racial and economic divides. There is a need to go deeper. However, it appears that this deeply religious community hope for some supernatural intervention as the words "God", "prayers" and "Church" were mentioned a number of times. Turning to God can sometimes be seen as some sort of escapism and not really committing to finding answers or avoiding confronting issues. Harry seem to be crying out for some practical steps that could be taken to heal the community. He has been around a long time and has talked to a lot of people, hence these utterances:

I think we have been talking about it for a long time. Yes, people say we are tired of talking about the same things. There are churches. They must come together and have conversations, including gangsters and police. People must have memories of these attempts to bring people together. Conversations must happen in the smaller towns. I request prayer and that everyone must pray, and I have an example about answered prayers.

There is always some awkwardness in the community development space when prayer is mentioned as something that can solve problems.

One of the participants mentioned how they have prayed for many years to see a revival so that things can come right while also expressing frustration that not much seems to be happening. Perhaps there is a case here regarding the place of religion and prayer in development.

It is well recorded that the church played a huge role in bringing about a new political dispensation in South Africa and how it was able to mobilize millions across the country to bring justice. Church facilities were often used for meetings.

It is probably for this reason than some participants feel that the church could still play a big role in terms of facilitating dialogues for social restitution.

Harry, who is a respected elder in a black community says the church does the heart work. He believes that the churches must win the hearts of their congregants. He emphatically states:

You see… to try to bring a change you must change from inside (heart) if you feel there is no justice you cannot bring change. I think the churches have not played their role. There are still white churches, you still have different residential areas for different economic brackets. Government has not been on board. Try to change the attitudes of the community.

The question around white guilt has come up. Some white participants said that the conversations could make them feel guilty. It is not uncommon for white people to feel guilty and in most cases, they don't know what to do with guilt. Suzanne seems to think that the church can deal with that, even though she admits that she is not a churchgoer and is not crazy about Christianity. She states the following:

> It is not the conversation that causes guilt. Guilt is there. I ask white people to listen, but they think I want them to feel guilty. Guilt is simmering there. Is Christianity not all about guilt and how you deal with it? The churches could play a more pro-active role.

Nobuntu, the woman at the Early Childhood Development centre, seems to point the finger at the church as well, hoping that help will come from there. It has been said that Sundays are the most segregated days of the week. The question that is being asked is whether churches play a role towards social cohesion? Nobuntu says:

> I think the ministers must be multiracial. There must be prayers because without prayers we cannot succeed. White domination.

Nobuntu is making an interesting link between church ministers, prayers and the notion of being multiracial, which could be called social cohesion, and then she adds that bit about white domination.

This again makes one think about how whites can contribute without dominating, even in conversations. Is there a place or a space where they can dominate? Regarding social restitution, who should lead? Perhaps whites must take a back seat, as they are a minority, so black leaders can step forward. However, it is about economic power and whites continue to control the economy.

It has often been said that charity begins at home. One could say that restitution begins at home. Of all the participants who saw a need for restitution and social cohesion in the town hardly anyone said anything about restitution at home except for one person:

> Restitution – the land issue, is it going to give me freedom? Where do we start if we want restitution? We need to start at the beginning, at home.

I am not sure how this would manifest itself at home, but I suppose if we seek sustainable peace and harmony at home, it would only be natural to want to see it beyond the confines of one's home. There is a case to be made about home life regarding seeking or pursuing a broader vision for the community, and indeed, the nation.

The participants kept mentioning a few names of people that they thought were the champions of racial harmony and social cohesion that could lead to social restitution. They were all white. It sounded right that white names were mentioned as champions, as they are members of a group that benefitted from a system that robbed others of fair treatment, dignity and self-emancipation. Jacobus mentioned the following people:

> Jacobus Ps, Jan Hans Stein, someone like yourself. Except for those two, Frank van Zyl is making the right moves. I know some people… in business. Ps Fanie and Helmut Pool given the right, and Deon Snyman.

I was taken by surprise and felt honoured when I was seen by Jacobus as one of the champions for social change and social restitution. It is of interest that they represent different spheres of society. Some of them are church ministers, a politician, a businessperson and a social entrepreneur.

Hilda says they seem to be struggling to see through honesty, even though she can see that efforts are being made. She makes the following observation:

Fanie is trying hard. They had a meeting with me. There is a difference in opinions. Also, they are struggling to see if people are honest and just window dress.

This raises the question of trust. Communities that have traditionally been on the opposite side of each other in an environment of injustice and oppression can never trust each other easily. It does appear that a trust building exercise could be one of the ways to enable communities to work hand-in-hand towards a common goal.

Trust is a big thing in community development work. It is always about the motives and whether the other person's motives are pure or not, and whose interests are being served. It is positive though that there is recognition that someone is trying and working hard.

The participants had different views about the apartheid spatial planning that has separated people according to race, thus making social cohesion and social restitution a challenge. There is a sense that this mentality that emanates from the apartheid social exclusion and separation has not been challenged.

The government continues to build townships on the periphery of cities and towns away from places of work and away from each other. The divide between communities is getting wider.

In Worcester, a new township is being built next to Zwelethemba Township; instead of building closer to town. But there is no clear solution to this, and Hilda seems to think there is a problem as she shares this:

A conversation that I had yesterday about people renting places in the upmarket areas to make them affordable – Durban Street is the divide. Affordable houses must be built. When people of colour move into a white space, whites move out. Municipality must also get involved.

She seems to suggest that even the affordability of houses does not solve the social cohesion challenge as whites begin to move away when people of colour move into these areas. She believes that there must be some involvement from the local government. The plea to be involved from government is a constant one. People see the need that goes beyond communities, probably some sort of pressure or force which has not been defined. The reason why white people move out varies; it is possibly 'fear of the unknown'. How many whites go to the township and see how the other half live? I know in Gauteng there was an initiative where white families spent a weekend in the township and black families spent the week-end in the 'white suburb'.

Jacobus weighs in on this by also challenging the apartheid spatial planning that is going on unchallenged even in the new political order. His take is the following:

> I think we are too sensitive. We have 100 employees who are looking for houses. Why do we build in separate areas? We need to deconstruct the apartheid mind-set. Government programme must provide social cohesion.

However, Henry in Zwelethemba sees things differently. He does not see a need for any government intervention. He can see that there have been changes and that some form of social cohesion is happening. He even raises his voice as he states the following:

> It depends on people. People can live anywhere. Coloureds and whites live here in the township. There is a new development here and everyone is free to apply. Things are different now. No more colour bar. This is a non-issue. Whites live in this township with black spouses. Coloured women go out with our young men. Nothing can ever change apartheid spatial planning.

Henry perhaps represents a view that is shared by some in his community. But he was the only participant who said that things are coming together, and that no effort ought to be made. I have not verified Henry's statement regarding whites and coloureds who live in Zwelethemba ,but I would not be surprised if there is a small number of them.

It has been expressed by participants that there must be some kind of government participation and that this cannot just be left to the communities to sort out on their own. The question of some government involvement can be a very tricky one because the dynamics of restitution are such that it is voluntary and therefore it cannot be forced on individuals. The issue of land expropriation without compensation is a burning one. Currently the government of South Africa is trying to intervene to solve the problem around land. It is a delicate one and has proved to be a difficult terrain for the government 25 years after democracy.

The participants, realizing the enormity of the challenge, expressed that this needs other interventions. Hilda expressed that she feels pain every day and stated the following:

> Its cruelty and 25 years later we still feel it. Things are not getting better. Government must get involved. The cruelty is still here. The problem is in the mind because we will know each other. Some people realize that it was cruelty. Some have changed and others have not.

It is an interesting choice of words by Hilda. She is the only one who expressed the current situation as "cruelty".

Judging by her body language and her voice tone, you could feel that the pain of being robbed of opportunities, the after effects of the bomb and thoughts about her future and children's future is a constant source of pain for her. There is a tendency to focus our thinking on what government at national level can do, but there might be a lot that government at local level could do.

One of the champions that was mentioned by the participant, a councilor, nudges the council in the right direction in terms of addressing inequality and creating space for social cohesion through the municipal facilities. Again, it is about resources or the lack of.

Jacobus is struggling with this as he verbalizes his thoughts around these provocative questions that have come up in conversations and what he has been exposed to. Then after a rather long speech, he says the following:

Sorry I am taking a lot of time. If it is justice or fairness, it was not a just game. What if someone were to say, there was no injustice? we need to try it to get right. I sometimes. You need to tip, can't catch up over time. We need to correct. Tipping the other way. How do you see that happen? Quota needs to be applied. Are the quotas for…….

I think there is a bigger question.

Whites must work harder now. Is everybody going to have the patience?

I can almost hear a sense of urgency in Jacobus's voice. It sounds like suddenly the lights came on and he is grasping the gravity of the situation.

He uses the phrases "we need to try to get it right", "We need to correct", "Tipping the other way" and "Quotas have to be applied…" This 'you hardly ever hear from white people', even to Jacobus it sounded like he was surprised to hear himself saying those things.

Then he talks about the bigger question. "Is everybody going to have the patience?" I could tell from the body language that he doubts it. He raises a critical question around sustainable peace when he asks whether people will be patient. I do think it is about Ubuntu and how it can be taught at schools so that people see that we are all equal.

A particularly important question to ask is: who must push the agenda for social restitution? Given our historical baggage and painful history of oppression and gross inequality where white people have access and control resources and the people of colour still feel the after effects of the policies of racial alienation and economic exclusion every day, I believe it should be white people.

The white people have allowed the new political order to unfold and have become participants by immersing themselves in political formations; ensuring that their interests are represented at a political level. The black political formations are seen to be representing black interests, so that is how things look in the political sphere.

But when you leave that sphere and come to the social sphere where millions are languishing in poverty, where there is lack of education and skills, lack of imagination and morale, and people in despair and without hope, it is different story Then in the middle of that, you have a prospering white community that is almost living in a bubble, detached from what is happening around their massive houses, high walls and gated housing complexes. Capitalism has also played a role as it has arguably made whites to want more, bigger houses, bigger cars etc. A different political system where people are recognized for their humanness or caring side rather than their wealth, is desirable and needed.

Jacobus is addressing Hilda's question around social restitution and restitution in general. Hilda feels that white people must know what to do and they shouldn't be asking her the question as it has often been the case in various settings. She simply asked. "Why must they ask me what they must do?"

The bigger question that needs to be looked at is to how to differentiate between restitution and charity. If white people do acts of charity at their own initiative, it could be seen as empty gestures that only serve to appease the conscience and as if they are projecting themselves as good Samaritans.

There are already many such initiatives happening in the country, but these do not lead to social cohesion and social justice and could, therefore not be classified as social restitution. Whites would have to give up some of their privilege and share wealth and resources with humility as an act of justice, not charity.

CHAPTER 12

Pathways to Social Restitution

LET'S TALK IT OUT:

The participants are very clear that there have to be talks and this is a feeling one gets from everyone. When one thinks about the new South Africa's political dispensation one reals that it was preceded by talks. Some of these talks were in secret and others in foreign lands.

However, nobody questioned the need for talks. There was even a time when there were "talks about talks".

There was a bit of caution, however, about talks that continue in perpetuity without producing any results. There must be a focus of the 'talks' to come up with credible solutions, such as having affordable housing in white areas and looking at equal education with equal resources.

Under this theme, it was expressed that these talks or conversations must be honest and sincere. There must be willingness to be genuine and vulnerable. This must not be a window dressing exercise. Part of this will have to be founded on an element of trust building. It is sometimes almost impossible to open up to people that you do not trust. This would be an important aspect since the divisions of the past have caused a great deal of distrust.

COURAGEOUS CONVERSATIONS WITHOUT INTIMIDATION

It was clear in the interviews that people did not want to talk openly on any platform because sometimes there are negative consequences for speaking your mind and talking about how you feel about things.

Although no space would feel 100% 'safe', at least an attempt has to be made, to create spaces where people are encouraged to be courageous.

COME LET US REASON TOGETHER

The learning here is on two levels. I see the formal learning that relates to the younger generation as a form of social emancipation.

It has been said that social restitution is not about here and now, it is about the future and how the next generation is being prepared for that future. In other words, education is laying the foundation for that future. Ali made it clear that he wants the quality of his learner's lives to be better, and for them to have an even brighter future than his.

LET US CONCRETIZE OUR CONVERSATIONS

The sub-theme seems to be relating to learning from each other through discussion. This formalized conversation could be facilitated through workshops.

A single identity workshop for those of the same race for group self-awareness exercises would be beneficial. This would then involve other races at a later stage, where practical outcomes could emerge.

WHO ARE THE DOERS AMONGST US?

In this subtheme, there is a need for practical examples where people can learn to do things.

A few names were mentioned of people who are seen to be doing social restitution. But it is a difficult thing as Suzanne expressed, almost in frustration, that it's something that you can't feel, touch or see.

This has come up many times when people have asked for examples of social restitution. There must be a list of examples that people can associate with social restitution, to learn from, use, and share. This cannot be a term that remains difficult to explain.

GOVERNMENT LET US DO IT TOGETHER

This subtheme relates to government learning from people or the other way round. The feeling is that it must be a collaborative effort. This would be at local government sphere, perhaps through the Integrated Development Plan where locals can influence policymaking and in turn, local citizen would get to learn how government functions.

GOD HELP US, WHERE IS THE CHURCH?

The role of the church featured very strongly. The reason may be the fact that members of WHRP are mainly churchgoers and therefore want to tap into what is called 'religious capital'.

Religious capital is often defined as the "skills and experiences specific to one's religion, including religious knowledge, familiarity with church ritual and doctrine, and friendships with fellow worshippers which produce religious resources that people define as valuable and explain religious behaviour."

Baker and Smith (2010) describe religious capital as "the practical contribution that faith groups make to society by creating networks of trust, guidance and support (e.g. through the use of a building, volunteers, paid community workers, training organizations and activities for a particular age or interest groups etc.) I think the people of Worcester would like to see the religious resources emanate from the church in different forms. The participants seem to be saying there is a great potential in the church, but it is seen as being inactive when it comes to releasing that potential.

In Worcester, there is a realization of that potential, especially among the ministers in the white Dutch Reformed Church. Some of them are very aware of the history of their church and how it was an integral part of endorsing past policies which Olwethu calls the "policies of cruelty".

It has been the experience of the researcher that churches sometimes tend to live in a bubble detached from the community. The participants are saying this must end and churches must provide direction and leadership on issues that affect the communities in which they are based.

AS FOR ME AND MY HOUSE

This subtheme was not very prominent, and it came out almost as a stand-alone point. Some participants seem to be associating church with family.

I do not necessarily share that view despite my own personal association with the church. The notion of charity beginning at home is behind this subtheme. However, traditionally churches have tended to be a support structure for families.

The message that the researcher would deduct from this is family as a support structure is important when one is involved in social restitution.

WE NEED MORE CHAMPIONS HERE

The participants mentioned the names of a few people in Worcester who seem to be championing the cause of social cohesion and social justice.

But there was a unanimous agreement that there are not enough people on the ground who have the necessary skills and influence to mobilize the critical mass so that a difference is made.

What the current champions are doing is enough evidence that if the numbers of such people were to grow, the impact would be visible.

WHITE PEOPLE, COME TO THE PARTY BIG TIME!

Social restitution means correcting or addressing the injustices of the past where a minority white government dominated the people of colour and a privileged status was carved out for themselves.

The white participants were quite explicit about the role their race played and are conscious of why their standard of living is different from the majority of Worcester who are black and coloured.

They stated that they feel guilty about it and are unsure of how to go about fixing things. Hilda was able to single out one white minister as someone who was trying very hard.

When Hilda was asked what she would say if white people were to ask her what they should do, she was silent for a moment and then asked a question of her own, "Why should they ask me?" Hilda was in fact saying that white people created the situation that we find ourselves in, so they should not be asking her how to fix it.

I am of the view that white people are often unsure of what to do and sometimes by trying to do something they make things worse. On the other hand, the people of colour do not want to carry the burden of having to tell white people what to do. And neither should they have to.

It appears that social restitution is a subtle message to white people to begin to discover and practice Ubuntu as described in this book. The participants would not have said it in so many words. It does however appear that it is what they want and hope for.

DELIVER US FROM BONDAGE

The participants agreed that they have not been freed from the past and the thinking is still very much framed by personal life experiences.

It has become normal to see people live in segregated spaces such as black townships, coloured townships and posh suburbs where whites live. Some coloured participants have admitted that in their community's black people are still seen as inferior. The racial hierarchy is still alive and well in the minds of many.

The blacks on the other hand have an issue of distrust when it comes to working with coloured people on issues of social importance. There is an acknowledgement that there must be a deconstruction of and renewal of the mind.

The participants did not seem to know how this could be done, but there is an inner yearning to become a community that thinks outside the box. This could be overcome by creating a vision for a new Worcester.

CHAPTER 13

Learning to change the world

P rofessor Njabulo Ndebele in his essay "Iph'indlela"-Finding your way through confusion, cites Muzi Khuzwayo as follows.

Muzi Khuzwayo, in the conclusion to his fine book, tells the story of how, a year before the 1999 elections, a 'white guy' who discovered that Muzi was in advertising came to him with a bizarre proposal. He sought advice on how to market a coffin-manufacturing company, which would flourish from the violence being anticipated at the time, and from all the HIV/AIDS deaths. As Muzi relates: "I refused to help him because I have faith in this country and its people. And every day the millions who get on buses, trains and taxis to go to work reaffirm my faith. Lately, the increasing crime, disease and interest rates are causing justified desperation. However, I still have faith. And faith does not have to be justified. My future depends on South Africans spending their hard-earned money on bread, books, alcohol, savings or investment accounts or anything else that keeps the economy going. If you are in marketing, advertising or any other industry, you must have faith. Irrational as it may be. Sometimes it will waiver and when that happens remember those people who stockpiled tons of food, water and petrol before our first democratic election. They were all wrong."

I, like Muzi, have faith in this country. I have come across so many people from both sides of the divide who are determined to *be the change* they want to see.

A friend of mine once showed me a beautiful letter that I have since shared with some of my friends about how privileged white South Africans can make a huge change in a community by reaching out to someone. Here is the letter to Sarah (not her real name)

Dearest Sarah,

Dale amazed me by showing genuine interest in knowing about the experiences of the people in Gugulethu and not only get to know but show a commitment to want to do something about their experience. Dale's visit to Gugulethu from time to time was always a breath of fresh air. I always remember your simple request to me during those uncertain times to please bring him back safely!

I often think of Dale's commitment to assist individuals that he can put a face to. His contribution in getting the church property fenced and buying the property on our behalf when white colleagues could not understand that black people were not allowed to own property in urban areas.

Dale went further by showing interest in my personal development as he paid for my doctoral studies at the University of Stellenbosch. I have fond memories of the many conversations we had. What I really miss are conversations with him whenever I listen to the changing face of our country especially with state capture etc. and wonder what he would have said…...

I recognise that there are many individuals from the privileged group of white people who have sought to reach out to bring positive change to others.

Some of my black friends are not really convinced that these efforts by our white compatriots are genuine. One can hardly blame them for feeling that way because of the levels of distrust cultivated by centuries of colonialism and decades of apartheid.

My wife Thandi and I attended Cornerstone Institute in Cape Town, mostly attracted by their motto - LEARN TO CHANGE THE WORLD.

I believe it is possible to have a better world, free of race-based inequality, free of social injustice and free of racism. I believe that we can all learn to change the world.

I am humbled by the knowledge that there can never be one single definitive way. There are many other possible paths that could lead to the fulfilment of my South African dream.

CITED SOURCES

- Couzens T " Battles of South Africa"
- De Grouchy J "I have come a long way"
- Diangelo R "White Fragility"
- Johnson P "Operation World '88"
- Mandela NR " Long walk to freedom"
- Mayekiso T "Exploratory Restitution Process in Worcester: The challenge for Development"
- Onyeani C "Capitalist Nigger"
- Peires J " The dead will arise: Nongqawuse and the great Xhosa cattle-killing movement of 1856
- Skosana X "The things we feel and dare not say "Disband the White Church"
- The Restitution Tool Kit
- Verwoerd W "My journey through family betrayals"

ABOUT THE AUTHOR

Theo can be found in various spaces actively engaged with the people around him. Whether it be in churches, organizations, community structures or public fora ,he pops up everywhere and wherever he surfaces he exudes love, care and empathy. He holds postgraduate degrees in Theology and Community Development. Theo is married and is the father of two.